The Fighter

A Spanish Civi

by

James R Jump

Edited by Jim Jump

with a Foreword by Paul Preston

The Clapton Press

About the author

James R Jump was a writer, teacher, linguist, poet and political activist whose life was shaped by his decision to fight in the Spanish Civil War. At the age of twenty-one he left his job as a newspaper reporter and travelled across France and the Pyrenees to join the International Brigades and risk his life in defence of the Spanish Republic. On returning to Britain, Jump married an anti-Franco Spanish refugee, served in the Royal Army Pay Corps and became a teacher. He was the author of several books on Spain and the Spanish language, beginning in 1951 with *The Spaniard and His Language* and ending with *The Penguin Spanish Dictionary*, published in the year of his death in 1990. His poems appeared regularly in *Tribune* and in several anthologies and collections.

Photograph from the author's International Brigade military carnet.

Contents

Contents (cont.)

The Fighter Fell in Love

I went to Spain to fight
for a cause,
to defend a people's right
to fair play and just laws.
I went resolved to fight.
I fought
and fell in love with Spain.

I went to Spain to fight
for an ideal,
so that her people might
enjoy justice – not imaginary but real.
I went to Spain to fight.
I fought
and fell in love.

I went to fight
in suffering Spain
against the two dictators' might.
I fought in vain.
I went resolved to fight.
I fought and lost
but I fell in love with Spain.

Foreword by Paul Preston

James Jump, known to his friends and comrades as 'Jimmy', was born in Wallasey, just over the Mersey from Liverpool whence came many volunteers in the International Brigades. His memoirs are atypical in several ways. Before leaving for Spain in November 1937, Jimmy was a journalist on the *Worthing Herald* and an aspiring poet. More unusually still, he could speak both French and Spanish. While there, he kept a diary, something that relatively few of his comrades did. In his typically generous appreciation of 'Jimmy', Jack Jones commented on the kindness, modesty and sensitivity that glows throughout this highly readable, informative and often exciting memoir. Bill Alexander, one-time commander of the British Battalion in the International Brigades, wrote: 'With different ideas and philosophy [Jim] could have achieved high status and rewards in the academic or literary fields.' But the course he took in joining the International Brigades 'was the only one at the time for those who cherished humanity and freedom'. Bill's words echo the moving inscription on the monument to the battalion on the South Bank of the Thames – a monument that Jimmy helped create – 'They went because their open eyes could see no other way' (a paraphrase of the lines from C Day Lewis's 1938 poem, *The Volunteer*: 'We came because our open eyes could see no other way'.

The Spanish war attracted many intellectuals and poets, but relatively few of them actually fought in the Brigades. Among those who did were the Oxbridge and London students such as John Cornford, Bernard Knox, Malcolm Dunbar and David Haden-Guest from Cambridge and Tom Wintringham, Ralph Fox, Lewis Clive, and Christopher Thornycroft from Oxford and Sam Lesser from London. By the time that Jimmy went into battle, on the Ebro in the summer of 1938, many were either dead or back home after suffering wounds. An important friend for Jimmy, after he was hospitalised out of the front line was one of the few remaining, his fellow poet, Miles Tomalin, a

Cambridge graduate.

An unusual aspect of these memoirs is that they have nothing to say about the early stages of the war and the International Brigade's role in the defence of Madrid, the battles of Jarama and Brunete. Jimmy went to Spain quite late, in November 1937, when things were looking ever bleaker for the Republic. When he and his companions reached Paris, they were surprised to find many other volunteers. While awaiting onward transport to the Spanish frontier, they visited the World's Fair, the great exhibition for which Picasso's *Guernica* had been commissioned by the Spanish Republican government. To find the relatively small Spanish pavilion, they had to pass the gigantic German and Russian pavilions. The Nazi pavilion, designed by Albert Speer, was a huge cubic mass, erected on stout pillars, guarded by naked Teutonic heroes and crowned by a gigantic eagle clutching a swastika in its claws. This architectural representation of Nazi aggression was faced, on the other side of the Trocadéro fountains, by the huge, thirty-three-feet high statues of an heroic Soviet couple, the man triumphantly brandishing a hammer and the woman a sickle. Jimmy and his companions were impressed by the Soviet installation and even more by the Republican one, of which he provides one of the best descriptions available. They were appalled by the British pavilion whose exhibits of golf-balls, pipes, fishing-rods, equestrian equipment and tennis rackets oozed the tired gentility of appeasement, in contrast with the German, Italian and Russian displays of military might. Jimmy and his comrades were greeted at the British pavilion by a larger-than-life-size, cut-out figure of Neville Chamberlain, fishing-rod in hand, wading in some Scottish salmon river. 'Oh Christ! Fancy putting that bastard in the exhibition,' said one of Jimmy's comrades.

The journey to Béziers near the Mediterranean coast, the time spent there and the exhausting crossing of the Pyrenees guided by French smugglers are vividly described. The joyous welcome by ordinary Spaniards is movingly recounted. The volunteers' train to IB headquarters in Albacete received a moving send-off. As it left the station at a snail's pace, 'someone started singing *The Internationale* and the crowd on the platform joined in'. The landscape that they passed through on their journey from the lush vegetation of Valencia into the arid slopes of Albacete is beautifully depicted in Jimmy's evocative prose. They reached Albacete on 15th November and immediately went on to the British Battalion's base in Tarazona de la Mancha. Because he spoke Spanish, Jimmy was posted as interpreter to a machine gun company. Already, half of the IB consisted of Spanish conscripts. His sheer usefulness kept Jimmy away from the front when he was promoted to interpreter at IB HQ. Accordingly, he was still at Tarazona when news came through of the capture of Teruel. A vital cog in the administration of the battalion, in quick succession, he was elevated to chief clerk and then paymaster. In early February, he was posted to the main IB HQ in Albacete as a clerk interpreter. He was thus deprived once more of, or saved from, active service at the front. The valuable pay-off for the reader is to get the hitherto untold story of the Brigades' routine administration, of how mail was distributed, how pay was organised, how personnel records were kept in the face of the rapidly changing details of the dead, the wounded, those captured and the few deserters. Far from being boring, these key details of how the battalion was run are recounted with humour.

Jimmy's gentle humour enlivens the text throughout. There are vivid character sketches such as that of Vicente Terol the whining, pale, pock-marked, records clerk, always scrounging cigarettes whose ambition was to have a safe cushy job as far from any fighting as possible. There are memorable evocations of civilian life behind the lines such as those of children playing at soldiers, parading through streets: 'They marched up and down, stamping their feet in time with the music from the loud-speakers. They had sticks which served as rifles and one of the oldest in the group drilled them, just as we had been drilled . . . There always seemed to be a toddler at the end of the column who fell over and burst into tears or who had to be reprimanded for his slowness. It was just like our training.'

On 22nd February, the news arrived of the Francoist recapture of Teruel. This was the prelude to Franco's great spring offensive, when 100,000 Nationalist troops swept through

Aragón and Castellón, reaching the Mediterranean by mid-April and splitting Republican Spain in two. When the Francoists captured Lérida, there was real alarm that they would soon reach the Mediterranean. The move of IB HQ to Barcelona – after tons of documents were burned – provides more insight about the rearguard. Their train passed through war-torn devastation north of Valencia, the consequence of constant bombing raids from Mallorca: 'There were bomb-craters in the fields near the railway track. Burnt-out wreckage of wagons, carriages and locomotives lay on both sides of the railway line. Alongside the road, which ran for miles parallel to the track, were smashed up lorries and cars. All the villages we went through were devoid of human life, though we saw stray dogs and cats in some.' Ending up in the village of Vilaseca, south of Tarragona, until 20th May, Jimmy helped organise a training camp there. At that time, he was shocked to learn of the execution of two Scandinavian deserters. His comment revealed humanity rather than the party line: 'Despite all that we had been told of defeatism, Trotskyism and fifth-columnists, I felt that these two men had really been executed merely because they were afraid and I wondered how afraid I would be when under fierce attack.'

Jimmy finally joined the British Battalion on 25th May 1938. The three 'British' companies overall contained about fifty per cent Spaniards. The rifle company to which he was posted consisted entirely of Spaniards apart from Jimmy himself. When his fluency in Spanish was noted, he became both an interpreter to a machine gun company as well as its secretary. For seven weeks from early June to 20th July, the XV Brigade was stationed near the town of Falset in Tarragona on the edge of the Priorat. The British and Irish, the Americans and Canadians bedded down in a dried up river bed to the east of the tiny village of Marçà alongside the road to La Torre de Fontaubella. Jimmy talks of the more energetic volunteers building shelters in case it rained. The resulting shanty town was nicknamed 'Chabola Valley', *chabola* being Spanish for the huts built from branches, canes and dried earth. Jimmy's account of the time spent there as the XV Brigade prepared to take part in the Republic's last great offensive is a valuable complement to Angela Jackson's *At the Margins of Mayhem. Prologue and Epilogue to the Last Great Battle of the Spanish Civil War.* Again, what he has to say about the non-military aspects of their sojourn is fascinating: 'There were also classes of a purely educational nature – to teach Spanish to those British volunteers who were interested, or to teach Spaniards how to read and write. There were many illiterate men among the conscripts.' Particularly interesting is what he has to say about the moral atmosphere within the Brigades: 'The political commissars were concerned not only with education, but also with the morale of the soldiers . . . on the look-out for signs of racialism, anti-semitism, drunkenness and sexual deviation, all of which were considered to be serious offences. Excessive drinking, like catching venereal disease, was looked upon as a danger not only to the individual but to the Spanish People's Army. The atmosphere was, in fact, quite puritanical. The official attitude to homosexual behaviour was even more severe.' Those caught could be transferred to a labour battalion.

In Marçà, the IB volunteers were visited by foreign dignitaries, none of whom could replicate the thrill that Jimmy had experienced when he had met Paul Robeson in Tarazona. If anything, the Brigaders were bored by eminent visitors such as 'Ellen Wilkinson (later to become Minister of Education in Attlee's post-war administration), Álvarez del Vayo (Foreign Minister of the Spanish Republic), Hewlett Johnson (the 'Red' Dean of Canterbury) and Earl Browder (Secretary of the US Communist Party).' Their efforts to encourage the men were expressed in nearly identical speeches replete with the same clichéd slogans which were wickedly mimicked later by the camp comedian. Jimmy at least liked Pandit Nehru, the future president of India, who mingled with troops.

Forces were being massed to mount a daring assault across the river Ebro in an attempt to restore contact between Catalonia and the rest of Republican Spain. It was thereby hoped to relieve the pressure on Valencia which was under ever greater threat from Franco's advance. The Nationalist lines were breached, although at great cost to the Brigades, heart-breakingly described in Jimmy's memoir. The initial crossing of the Ebro towards

Gandesa was relatively easy. They encountered the first signs of Francoist resistance after they reached Corbera. By then, Francoist reinforcements were being rushed in. The struggle to capture Gandesa was Jimmy's first battlefield action. The fear that he experienced under heavy artillery and aerial bombardment is revealed honestly. He realises that he 'would never make a real soldier' and, with harsh self-criticism, 'came to the conclusion that I was only intellectually an anti-fascist. I knew that fascism was evil. All that I had read convinced me that under a Nazi or fascist regime the individual would count for nothing. But this anti-fascist feeling came from the head, not the guts. Politically speaking, I sometimes felt almost ashamed of myself and my thoughts. All around me were men who had suffered poverty and unemployment, and the degradation that accompanied those two evils. These men were capable of hatred and revenge. To them, fascism was an extension of capitalism, under which they had suffered hardship and humiliation. They were coal-miners from Scotland and South Wales, hunger-marchers from the shipyards of the North-East, Irish Republicans who felt that their cause had been betrayed by De Valera. They had not become socialists through reading *Left Review* or the *New Statesman*.'

Like other memoirs before this one, we have here another stark reminder of the horrors undergone by Republican soldiers during the constant bombardments as they resisted on bare hillsides with little shelter from the blazing sun. Jimmy pays moving tributes to the bravery of those who died. They were short of food and water. Despite the suffocating heat, priority for water had to be given to cooling the machine guns: 'Although we had enough ammunition, we had hardly any equipment. Most of us were bare-headed, dressed in shirts and trousers. Few had boots. Most of us wore sandals or rope-soled *alpargatas*. I doubt if there were more than four steel helmets in the whole company. We had no pouches, but carried our ammunition in our pockets or in bags tied to our belts.' It was almost impossible to bury the dead and life took place amid the stench of putrefying corpses. Men died from wounds and others went mad with shell-shock. Jimmy was reluctantly hospitalised from 30th August to 23rd

September after collapsing with jaundice.

When Jimmy's unit was pushed back across the Ebro along with the rest of the Popular Army, it was the end for the Republic. While he was still in hospital, in the vain hope of securing international support, Juan Negrín, the Republic's prime minister, unilaterally withdrew the volunteers. Jimmy missed the formal farewell parade held in Barcelona for them at the end of October 1938 although he recalls the heart-rending descriptions given him by comrades of the moving reception given them by ordinary people. He captures precisely the sense of disorientation felt by men who had fought and suffered for an ideal, without expectation of reward. They had stayed on in the hope of victory for the Republic but now faced, at best, an uncertain future. He provides one of the best explanations of the volunteers' repatriation: 'The "official line" was that the Spanish People's Army was now strong enough to fight alone without foreigners. I thought that the government's decision was simply an act of compassion. The leaders knew that the war was lost and that if we were captured we would almost certainly be shot. Therefore they decided to send us home where, at least, we would be useful propagandists against fascism.'

Jimmy was not demobbed until 25th November. He provides a moving account of the journey home and the emotional support from both Spanish and French civilians who greeted the volunteers' train as it passed. Equally moving is his portrayal of the riotous welcome that they received on arriving at Victoria Station. There, the memoirs come to a sudden end, when Jimmy is met by his brother who gives him the news that his father has just died.

The rest of Jimmy's life is given in a brief but informative account by his son, Jim. He muses: 'Why was Jump's memoir not published while the author was still alive? No correspondence or other clues are to be found in his papers, but I suspect that my father didn't try that hard. This would have been especially likely in the 1960s and 1970s, when interest in the International Brigades was relatively modest.' Given that Jimmy, although deeply committed to the Republican cause, was open-minded, he was not frightened to write of executions for desertion or for alleged Trotskyism. That being the case, I think it was more likely that comrades of the International Brigade Association would have been uncomfortable with his candid discussion of such issues. If Jimmy was inhibited about this, he should not have been, for his memoirs recreate the camaraderie, idealism and stoicism of his fellow volunteers as well as the misery of defeat. In that regard, they have much in common with another important memoir by a British volunteer, Fred Thomas's *To Tilt at Windmills*. Much of the value to historians of *The Fighter Fell in Love* derives from its basis in a perceptive diary.

What shines through this self-deprecating, painfully honest and brutally realistic memoir is a writer with a poet's eye for detail, a gentle sense of humour and, above all, the intelligence of a thoroughly decent man. I was amused to note that he had written: 'Five years ago, when I was living in Spain, I was asked by a London publisher if I could write a school text book with the title *How Spain Is Run*. I replied that I could do it in three words: "Corruptly and inefficiently".' Having spent years writing a book on corruption and political incompetence in Spain, and sharing with him a love of the country and its people, this just made me wish I had known him better.

* * * * *

Sir Paul Preston is Emeritus Professor of Spanish History at the London School of Economics and Political Science. He is the author of many books on Spain and the Spanish Civil War. His latest is *A People Betrayed: A History of Corruption, Political Incompetence and Social Division in Modern Spain 1874-2018* (2020).

Preface by Jack Jones

Half a century has passed since the war in Spain was at its height, yet there is much interest in the events of the war amongst people in all parts of the world. This is especially the case with the activities of the International Brigades. In response to the call to defend the democratically elected government under devastating attack from international fascism, men wended their way to Spain from many countries; young men for the most part and one of the youngest from Britain was the author of this book.

The human side of the story has too often been overlooked or obscured in written accounts and records of the international volunteers. Jimmy Jump repairs that omission in a very readable fashion. He is especially qualified to do so. When the author went to Spain, although quite young, he had already had some journalistic experience and he managed to keep something of a diary; moreover he knew Spanish. But it is the nature of the man which stands out in this book. His kindly, modest, sensitive character impresses even today.

Experiences and responses varied greatly among the volunteer fraternity who fought for the Spanish Republic, leaving home and loved ones to serve in a foreign land in the cause of principle. This sketch of life in Spain fills out some of the human background, in vivid and moving terms, of those far-off days. It gives the lie to those who have maligned the volunteers as 'mercenaries' or 'tools of Moscow'. An instinctive sense of solidarity, fairness and humanity is apparent throughout these pages.

Jimmy Jump reveals that he was not always at ease with harsh decisions, but his dedication and commitment to the cause of freedom and the defeat of fascism remained firm throughout, as was the case with the overwhelming majority of those who served in the International Brigades. Hardship was suffered and life was indeed serious but there were many humorous, lively and light-hearted moments which Jimmy illustrates so well in this volume, embellished with some splendid poetry. These verses of his typify much of the poetry he has written in recent years and for which he is held in high regard by the veterans of the International Brigades still living in Britain and Ireland.

I thoroughly enjoyed reading this book and not only because it evoked a little nostalgia. It is a real pleasure to commend it as a worthy contribution to the literature of the Spanish war.

* * * * *

Jack Jones (1913-2009) was a Liverpool docker and Labour councillor when he went to Spain in 1938 to join the International Brigades. Wounded in the Battle of the Ebro, he returned home and rose through the ranks of the Transport & General Workers' Union to become its general secretary from 1968. Following retirement ten years later he became president of the National Pensioners' Convention and in 2001 the founding life president of the International Brigade Memorial Trust. This preface was written for the second version of James R Jump's memoir in 1987.

Note on place names

For consistency and in line with the original manuscripts, all place names in Catalonia are in Spanish rather than the now more commonly used Catalan.

Chapter 1 : Preparations
The weeks up to 6 November 1937

What I was planning to do was illegal. I discovered this when I applied to the Foreign Office for a passport application form. The form arrived together with a printed note stating that all passports issued would be stamped 'Not valid for Spain'. I decided that, if I could not go to Spain legally, I would go illegally. I spoke first to Margaret Elliott, a fellow member of the Worthing Labour League of Youth. Margaret's brother Tom had gone to Spain at the beginning of 1937 and, although more than eight months had elapsed, no word had been heard from him, not even a postcard. Margaret and her parents were now resigned to the idea that he was dead and much later it was confirmed that he had been killed at Jarama.[1]

'How did he travel to Spain?' I asked her.

'He went quite openly with a passport. At that time there were no restrictions on travel to Spain.' Margaret added that she knew of no organisation that would help me.

Next I thought of Dorothy Thornycroft, who lived in a large house in Broadwater, on the outskirts of Worthing. Perhaps she could help me for, besides being active in most left-wing causes, her own son Christopher had dropped out of university to go to Spain. I knew Dorothy quite well as she was the leading light on the committee that ran the two local homes for Basque refugee children.[2]

She met me in the restaurant above the cinema in the centre of Worthing. Over coffee and biscuits she implored me not to go to Spain. 'Think of your mother and father,' she pleaded. 'You cannot imagine how they will suffer, worrying for your safety. I know because I have experienced it.'

I told her that my mind was made up. I was determined to go. She used every kind of argument to try to dissuade me, even telling me that the previous evening I had been co-opted to the Basque children's committee. When she saw that I would not change my mind she said, sadly: 'If you are quite determined, then see Joe Matthews. He could put you in touch with the right people.'

Matthews, a conscientious objector in the First World War, was the secretary of the Worthing branch of the Communist Party.[3] I knew him fairly well. We were both members of the Labour Party's anti-fascist committee, the only Labour organisation allowed to collaborate with communists and members of other parties.

I wrote to him and he came to see me at my digs.

'I want to go to Spain and join the International Brigade,' I said bluntly.

'Good for you,' Joe answered. 'If I were younger I'd be tempted to do the same thing myself.'

'But where do I go? I can't get a passport and go legally.'

'I'll give you a letter of introduction,' he answered. 'Have you an envelope and some paper?' There and then he wrote a short letter and told me the address in London where I should take it.

The following Saturday afternoon found me sitting on a hard chair in a dingy London office. I was being interviewed by a middle-aged man who smoked incessantly, stubbing out his cigarettes in one of two ashtrays that were already overflowing onto the untidy desk.[4]

I presented the letter of introduction, which he read carefully. 'Your mind is made up, comrade?' The word 'comrade' came from his lips quite naturally. Back in Worthing we had used the term shyly, with almost a conspiratorial air.

'Yes,' I replied. 'That's why I'm here.'

'You're not running off to Spain to escape from the police, or anything like that?'

'No.'

'I hope you realise you have to go for the duration of the war, or until the Spanish government discharges you.' He paused to light another cigarette and then went on. 'At first we recruited comrades for nine months or a year, after which they were brought home. We don't do this anymore.'

'I understand.'

'Is there anything you'd like to tell me about yourself?' he asked.

'I speak Spanish. I learned it at school and recently I've been getting a lot of practice. I also speak French.'

'Good, that'll be useful, because the British Battalion is not all British. About half are Spaniards.'

'Oh, really.' This was something I was not aware of.

'Have you ever been abroad?' he asked.

'Yes. Once to Paris.' I did not add that I had gone, at the age of twelve, with a school party.

My interrogator stood up and, smiling, said: 'We shall accept you. I want you to come back here Saturday afternoon at half-past three, ready to travel. Don't bring a lot of luggage. You can't drag a suitcase across the Pyrenees. In any case, you have to look like a weekend tripper to Paris.' We shook hands and I left.

Back in Sussex, when the news leaked out that I was leaving I was naturally asked many questions. I was working at the time as a reporter with the *Worthing Herald*, so I let it be thought that I was returning to my native Merseyside to work on a newspaper there.

At the Basque children's home in Lancing, where I was a frequent visitor (my fiancée, Cayetana, was one of the helpers there) I announced that I was going back to Liverpool. I thought my story was believed, until the time came for me to say '*Adiós*'. I shook hands with all the staff, Fernando and Rosa Omegna,[5] Concha, Mari, and Felisa. When I shook hands with Felisa, she slipped a piece of paper into my hand and whispered: 'My sister's address. Call on her if you can. She will be very happy.' Outside, I unfolded the piece of paper, which had an address in Spain. It occurred to me that I was not a convincing liar after all.

On Saturday 6th November I was once again in the untidy recruiting office, where I met the four men who were to be my travelling companions. We sat on bent wooden chairs in a half-circle facing the chain-smoker behind the scruffy desk. Behind him on the wall was a large map of Spain fastened by pins. The front line was marked by a piece of thin red tape which wound its irregular course across the peninsula. From the mountains in the north it took a hairpin bend round Teruel, swept through the

23

suburbs of Madrid and finally reached the Mediterranean coast near Málaga.

'Have you all made up your minds? Do you realise that you will receive less pay than Spanish soldiers? After all they may have families to maintain. Do you accept these conditions?'

Yes, we accepted them but said nothing, we merely nodded.

'Then, there's nothing more to be said, comrades.'

We stood up, ready to go, and the man turned to me. 'As you speak French and Spanish I'm making you leader of this group. You will be responsible for their safe arrival at the Spanish frontier.'

He offered me a cigarette and lit it himself. He took a deep puff and then continued: 'Here are your instructions. The five of you must stick together, but you must not talk to members of any other group, even though you are certain that their destination is the same as yours. I hope that's quite clear.'

He took out a black metal cash-box from the top drawer of his desk and handed me eighteen pounds in cash and silver. 'This will be plenty to pay for your fares to Paris and to buy meals and cigarettes for the journey.'

I pocketed the money. 'And when we get to Paris, what do we do then?' I asked.

He replied by handing me a slip of paper bearing an address in the Place du Combat.[6] 'You will go to this address, ask for Max and say that Jack has sent you.'

I repeated the instructions and he appeared satisfied. I left the office and told my four travelling companions to meet me under the clock in Victoria Station at half-past nine that night. Then there only remained the goodbyes to be said to Cayetana, who had been waiting with a friend in a nearby café.

The fog outside was quite thick when we all met at the station. I purchased the tickets and we joined the queue before the barrier at the end of the platform where the boat-train was waiting. As we slowly approached the barrier I noticed that behind the ticket inspector examining the tickets was a man in plain-clothes who was scrutinising all the travellers. We guessed he was a policeman. We presented our tickets and, as I had feared, we were stopped by the policeman.

'Where are you going?'

'To Paris,' I replied and added innocently: 'This is the right train isn't it?'

'What is the purpose of your visit to France?'

'We're off to visit the International Exhibition.'[7]

'You're not thinking of going to Spain?' he questioned.

'Certainly not!' I answered. The policeman looked quite unconvinced, but we were allowed to board the train.

Once we had found a compartment on the train we told each other our names and I was able to look at my travelling companions and take stock of them. I realised that I was easily the youngest of the group.

The two older men were Mac, who said he was from Glasgow and a ship's radio operator, and Leonard Denny, who had a pronounced Liverpool accent.[8] Neither was very talkative, though Denny did roll up his right trouser leg to show us the scar of a wound that he said he had received on the Somme. While he was willing to talk about his military experience, he told us nothing about his more recent life, neither what his job was, nor the circumstances which had led him to join the International Brigades. I had the impression that he and Mac wanted to leave Britain at the earliest possible moment and that he would have joined the French Foreign Legion or escaped to South America if he had been given the opportunity.

If Leonard Denny and Mac were uncommunicative, Billy, from Northern Ireland, was the exact opposite, entertaining us throughout the journey. He told us that he had been in Spain for six months during the earlier fighting and had returned to Britain after being wounded. He kept us engrossed with his stories, whether they were true or not, of the battles at Jarama and Brunete, of Moorish troops who carried curved knives, of German dive-bombers and of the tortures to which International Brigaders were subjected if they were taken prisoner by the fascists.[9]

He gave us one piece of very sound advice. 'Don't throw away your cigarette-ends. Tobacco's like gold dust in Spain,' he explained, 'soap, chocolate and razor-blades, too,' I had indeed noticed that he carefully saved the tobacco from all his cigarette-ends in a metal tobacco tin.

The name of the other volunteer escapes me. He was well-spoken and obviously well-educated, though with an aloof and superior manner; he could have been a civil servant, a teacher or an office worker.

The journey to France was quite uneventful. We saw various other groups on the train and on the channel steamer, but made no contact with them.

When we were approaching the French coast I left my four companions, who were playing cards, and went on deck. A man of about my own age came and leaned on the rail by my side. We talked of the weather, the Paris exhibition and other 'safe' topics. Suddenly he said: 'I'm going to Spain. Are you?'

I was somewhat taken aback by the suddenness of his question and remembered what I had been told about *agents-provocateurs*. Instead of answering his question, I countered with another. 'Why are you going to Spain?'

'I'm going to fight against Franco and his bloody communists.' There was no answer to this. Surely he could not possibly be a police spy. Wouldn't the authorities employ someone with a little more knowledge of the Spanish political situation? I did not tell him that I too was on my way to Spain.

He kept on talking. He told me that he came from Blackburn, where he had been working as a waiter. He was a Roman Catholic, and his name was Joe Moran. He was also someone whom I would meet again in Spain.

After a while I left the rail and returned to my companions. After a meal on the boat, on Billy's advice we decided to buy some more cigarettes. 'In Spain, if you have tobacco you're a millionaire, believe me,' he said.

None of us carried any luggage. Before leaving my lodgings in Worthing I had simply put into my pockets my shaving gear, a comb, a toothbrush, some soap and a silver-handled penknife, which my colleagues on the *Worthing Herald* had presented to me, and a photo of Cayetana.

International Brigaders

'I compare the International Brigades to modern Don Quixotes
in a world of Sancho Panzas.' – *Fernando Sanz Compán,*
Liverpool correspondent of a number of Spanish newspapers
before and during the Spanish Civil War

Five brigades of Sorrowful Knights,
liberty their Lady Dulcinea,
pitting their pitiful weapons,
daring to put up a fight,
against the overwhelming might
of the four great Sancho Panzas,
the general, the landowner, the bishop and the banker
and their loyal servants,
despotism, superstition, threats and treachery.

Five brigades of Sorrowful Knights,
confident that, even against all odds,
though they might lose the battle in Spain,
they will win the war in the world.

Chapter 2 : Paris
7-8 November 1937

The train pulled up in the Gare du Nord just before daybreak on 7th November. We shivered with cold as we left the warm, stale air of the compartment, and I suggested having breakfast. Soon we were standing at the bar of a nearby café enjoying fresh croissants washed down with hot coffee.

Next we piled into a taxi. I told the driver the address in the Place du Combat which I had been given and he nodded, saying that he knew the place. We soon stopped outside a door in a high wall.

'It looks like a prison,' commented Mac.

I paid the taxi-driver, but when I tried to give him a tip, he shook his head in refusal. '*Bon voyage et bonne chance, camarades!*' he said. As he drove away he raised a clenched fist and shouted: '*¡Salud!*'

At the address given to me I had to ask for Max and say that Jack had sent us. I did so; the door in a long blank wall opened and we were admitted to a large hall full of groups of men seated on benches waiting to be interviewed and medically examined. We were told to sit down and wait. My ears caught the sounds of German, Italian, French and American English, but there were other languages that I did not recognise.

It was clear that not everyone there was going to join the Spanish army. There were injured men, some with arms and legs missing, who were returning from Spain. A man of about thirty detached himself from one of these groups and came over to us. He spoke with a cockney accent. 'Are you on your way out to Spain?' he asked.

'Yes,' I replied.

'Suckers,' he said.

We were taken aback by the suddenness of all this and he must have seen this reflected in the expressions on our faces, for he went on: 'It wasn't too bad in the early days. There was plenty of food, and plenty to drink and smoke. But it's just hell now. Christ, I'll be glad to get back to London.'

He then turned and walked back to his friends.

Before we could think about what we had been told, a middle-aged man, French, I think, joined us. He spoke almost perfect English. First he asked us to turn out our pockets. We did so and he took most of the money we had left. Billy and Mac protested. I asked why he was taking our money.

'Don't worry,' he replied. 'You'll be so well looked after that you won't need a lot of money. You see, we don't want you to do anything foolish. Paris is full of police spies, and men who drink too much talk too much. Only last week we sent two men back to England. Also, we don't want to send you to Spain with a dose of syphilis. You'll end up in a Spanish gaol, not the Spanish army.

'Now to business,' he said, beckoning us to a nearby table. 'Come here, one of you.' As group leader, I was the first to sit down and answer his questions.

'Name?'

'James Robert Jump.'

'Age?'

'Twenty-one.'

'Where were you born?'

'Wallasey, Cheshire.'

'Nationality?'

'British.'

'Occupation?'

'Newspaper reporter.'

'Next of kin?' I told him my father's name and address.

One by one we answered his questions, after which he again spoke to us as a group. We were told that we would be in Paris for one night, and were given the name of a hotel nearby and tickets which would entitle us to eat in a co-operative restaurant. We were free to go wherever we wished in Paris, but we were advised to behave like ordinary tourists.

Finally our interviewer said: 'If any of you feel that you cannot go ahead with this, don't be ashamed to tell us now. You will be given a ticket back to London, and we shall ask no questions.' There was a pause, and we looked at one another,

We Cannot Go Back

We cannot go back to the old way of life,
the life that we lived before;
for the slaughter of innocents makes us think
of war.

Those habits we had seemed all right to us then,
but will not return again,
for we cannot forget those things we learned
in Spain.

When the cowards come up against Hitler's advance
they retreat, to his delight.
But the people of Spain are not made that way.
They fight.

They've taught us that Fascism can be stopped,
we must defend what is right;
and they've shown us the easiest way to win:
Unite!

We've been taught (by a country called 'backward')
that Fascists do not give in
and our comrades must die in the fight before
we win.

Santa Coloma de Farnés, 16th October 1938

Chapter 3 : Béziers and the long march
9-11 November 1937

When I awoke it was beginning to get light and I caught glimpses of the Mediterranean. That, in itself, was a thrill, as I had never been so far from home before. I looked at my watch, but I had forgotten to wind it up. It had stopped at half-past two. The sky was red, and I wondered if 'red sky in the morning' meant bad weather in the south of France.

The train pulled in at Béziers and I saw by the station clock that it was just after seven. I asked the ticket collector how to get to our hotel and he advised us to take a taxi. As we drove through the town the café owners were already putting out tables and chairs on the pavements, as if expecting a fine day. The streets were clean, unlike those of the district of Paris where we had stayed, with colourful flower-pots on window-ledges and multicoloured sun-blinds and awnings everywhere.

Our hotel was situated in one of the main streets. The landlady was a plump, smiling, middle-aged woman who spoke a little Spanish. She showed us to our rooms, and we felt the soft feather mattresses in anticipation of a good night's sleep.

'You must be hungry,' said madame. 'You can have breakfast whenever you want, either inside the café or at the table on the terrace.'

After a quick wash and shave we went down to the café, where we were served with enormous bowls, holding at least half a litre of milky coffee. There was also a plate piled with warm croissants. We had hardly begun to eat when a young man dressed in blue overalls cycled up to the café, leaned his bicycle against the kerb and entered. He glanced quickly at all the patrons, and then came and sat at our table. '*Bonjour, camarades,*' he began. 'Does anyone speak French or Spanish?'

'Yes,' I said.

In a mixture of Spanish and French our contact said we would be in Béziers for at least two days, possibly three or four. 'It is necessary that you spend your time here resting,' he added.

'When you leave here you must walk across the Pyrenees. That is difficult and tiring enough in summer. In November, and at night . . .'

He had no need to finish the sentence. We all guessed what he meant.

'Ask him how long it takes,' said Leonard Denny. 'I'm not as young as I was.'

He must have guessed what Leonard had asked, or he knew a little English, for he did not wait for me to translate.

'One cannot say. With luck you should reach Spain after six hours, but if there is mist or snow, the journey could lengthen to twelve hours or even more. So you will understand how important it is for you to rest and eat well while you are here. You will receive your next instructions either from us or from madame. You are free to move about Béziers, but please be in this hotel, or near it, by five o'clock each evening.'

Our first day in Béziers was a pleasant one. Although it was November, the sun shone brightly and the weather was warm. We strolled through the streets, sat on benches in public gardens and drank beer on the terrace of the café beneath the hotel. Billy continued to salvage the tobacco from all his cigarette-ends, and I started surreptitiously, and rather ashamedly, doing the same. We spoke to no strangers unnecessarily.

That night Mac disappeared. When he did not get up for breakfast on the morning of 10th November, we went to his room and saw that his bed had not been slept in. A search revealed that he had taken his belongings. I went immediately to the landlady and informed her. She looked worried and went off to make a telephone call.

'This is bad,' she said to us when she returned to our table. 'I have told the young man who was here yesterday.'

Mac's disappearance worried us too. All morning we expected at any moment to be picked up by the police. At midday we were in our rooms, waiting to eat, when our contact of the previous day returned. He told us that the disappearance of one of our group could be serious. If he had been arrested by the police, we might find ourselves in serious trouble. 'Do you know anything about him?'

'Nothing much,' I answered. 'He said that he was a ship's radio operator.'

'Ah, then maybe he has decided to make his way to Marseilles, to pick up a ship there. But we must be ready for the worst. If the police come round here, you must not speak. Answer no questions. The landlady will let us know, and the "organisation" will look after you.'

In the afternoon we visited the zoo and returned to the hotel at about five, just as our contact cycled up. 'You are leaving here this evening,' he told us. 'Please be ready to depart in about an hour's time.' It was half-past six when we were bundled into a battered old taxi and driven off. It soon grew quite dark and we had no idea how many towns and villages we went through in the next two hours.

Suddenly, at a little before nine o'clock, the taxi turned sharply to the right along a short, bumpy lane and pulled up in a farmyard. Someone guided us to a door, through the cracks of which lines of light were shining. I pushed open the door and, for a second or two, we stood there dazzled by the brightness inside.

We found ourselves in a large barn filled with trestle-tables, at which dozens of men were seated. Some were busy eating; others, who had been there longer and had finished their meal, were talking and smoking. There was a group in one corner singing to the accompaniment of a guitar.

'Sit down and eat, comrades,' a young woman told us.

We were looking for four vacant places when I heard a voice I recognised calling me. 'Hi there, Limey! So you made it at last.' It was Larry, the American I had met in Paris who had arrived on the *Queen Mary*.[11]

I sat next to him and started to eat. I don't know how old Larry was, but he looked no more than sixteen or seventeen. He was only about five feet tall and he had a high-pitched, cracked voice like a boy's voice that is just breaking. I was not really hungry, but the bread was fresh, the cooked meats delicious and the coffee hot.

'Where are you from?' I asked Larry.

'Milwaukee.'

'That's near Chicago, isn't it?'

37

'Uh-huh. You?'

'My home's near Liverpool, but I've been working in Sussex.'

'Gee, those English names really get me – Sussex, Devon, Yorkshire' (he made the second syllable rhyme with 'fire'). 'My grandpop came to the States from Nottingham, you know, the place Robin Hood came from. When I was a kid he gave me a book about Robin Hood. I'd like to go there some time and see the forest. Is it still there?'

'Yes, I think so.'

We chatted about the war in Spain and discussed the policies of Franklin Roosevelt and Neville Chamberlain. Finally we got round to books.

'I recently read Upton Sinclair's novel *The Jungle*, about the Chicago meat-packing industry,' I told him. 'Uh-huh.' Larry sounded as though he had never heard of it.

'And I enjoy Sinclair Lewis's books, especially *Elmore Gantry* and *Babbitt*.' Larry's only comment was another non-committal 'uh-huh', so I tried another tack. 'What do you think of the negro poet Langston Hughes?'

'I ain't read him. I'm not stuck on poems.'

'Which American writers do you read? Who are the leading writers of the present day?' I persisted.

'Earl Browder and William Z Foster.' (The initial was pronounced 'zee'.) Now it was my turn to say 'uh-huh', as I had never heard of Browder nor Foster. Much later I discovered that they were the secretary and chairman of the US Communist Party – fluent orators, but hardly literary giants.

Larry and I swapped cigarettes, Players for Camels. I felt good, with a full stomach.

* * * * *

There must have been men of at least a dozen different nationalities in the barn. They wandered from one group to another trying out their French, German, English, Italian. Two New Yorkers were holding a conversation of sorts with a German. He spoke German, they spoke Yiddish. There was an atmosphere of camaraderie.

Mine had been the last group to arrive. We were urged to eat more, even though we were satisfied. 'You have a long motor-drive before you, and after that an even longer walk,' we were told.

Soon the order came to leave. We shook hands with the French family who had served the meal and climbed into three motor-coaches. All the blinds were drawn, so we had no idea where we were being taken. We drove for about two hours, passing through two towns (we could hear the traffic) and during the last hour noticed that the coach was climbing steadily and negotiating many sharp bends.

It must have been close on midnight when we alighted in a narrow, tree-lined lane. Before the coaches drove away we saw our three guides emerge from a copse. Each carried a sack which he emptied on the ground, and I made my first acquaintance with *alpargatas* – canvas shoes with inch-thick rope soles, which were at that time worn by all Spanish peasants and many townsfolk.

The guides told us in a mixture of French and Spanish to take off our shoes and put on the *alpargatas*. They said that they were silent and would enable us to climb over smooth, wet rocks without slipping. With our shoes in our raincoat pockets, or tied by the laces and hanging round our necks, we set off, in single file, led by two of the guides. These men, we discovered, were smugglers, the famous Spanish *contrabandistas* who knew every track in the Pyrenees as a London taxi-driver knows the streets of his city. The 'organisation' employed them to smuggle volunteers into Spain – contrary to the orders of the League of Nations' Non-Intervention Committee.[12]

Our guides led us down the road for about twenty yards and then turned left along a narrow track through the trees, and up a fairly steep slope. The night was dark and I could see hardly anything except the vague shape of the man in front of me. I soon discovered that the *alpargatas* were all that the guide had claimed. The ground was wet, as though it had rained not long before, and we continued to climb, but the guides set a fast pace and we just had to follow. Soon I was aglow and perspiring, in spite of the chill night. I felt sorry for some of the older men – I guessed that they were in their early forties – although they were in a minority. Most of the volunteers that I had seen in the barn were in their twenties.

There was no moon but, even if there had been enough light, I was too busy keeping close to the man ahead of me to gaze at the scenery. Perhaps that was as well, for I have no head for heights and who knows how terrified I might have been had I been able to view the depth of the gorges we skirted.

The journey seemed endless – up the steep hill that lay ahead of us, a short descent, and then up an even steeper slope. This was the pattern, repeated time after time. God knows how many slopes we panted up only to see, on reaching the summit, the black silhouette of an even higher one half a mile ahead.

There were only two breaks. After about an hour and a half we were allowed a short rest. We could not smoke, and could only talk in whispers, but we ate some of the bread and meat which we had brought with us from the barn. Then at a signal from one of the guides, we resumed our arduous march.

At about three o'clock in the morning we halted again. Our route crossed a road. One at a time, when one of the guides tapped us on the shoulder, we ran across the road and waited among the trees on the other side. The operation stopped for a while, just before it was my turn, when a vehicle was heard approaching. From the sound, it was a motorcycle and we all wondered if it was a policeman deployed to uphold the French government's ban on foreign volunteers going to Spain. When the motorcyclist passed we all breathed more easily.

A little later we heard dogs barking, and wondered if the police used dogs to guard the routes into Spain, but our guides seemed unconcerned. The scrambling up and down mountain tracks continued and I was beginning to wonder if I would be able to go on much longer without a rest. Panting and with a tight chest, I was wet with perspiration and my feet were soaked through as I had stepped inadvertently into a mountain stream. Then, with a suddenness that shook us out of our thoughts, the guide at the rear shouted at the top of his voice. *'¡Ya estamos, camaradas! ¡Estamos en España!'* (We're now in Spain, comrades. We're in Spain.) It was 11th November, less than five days since setting off from London.

The column halted and we sat on the wet ground, laughing, talking, smoking. Some of the Germans started singing revolutionary songs, ending with *The Internationale*, which we all joined in.

Suddenly we felt less weary. I had had the childish idea that, on reaching the summit of the next hill, we would see before us a vast plain of green fields and white-washed houses with red tiled roofs – the picture of rural Spain that I had imagined. I was disappointed, therefore, to find that the mountains continued. In fact the Spanish slopes seemed even steeper.

We resumed our march and soon saw that the sky to our left was tinged with yellow. Dawn was approaching, and the knowledge that we were in Spain gave extra strength to our aching thigh and calf muscles. Now we could shout, sing and joke, and the climbing up and scrambling down, the stumbling over jagged rocks and plunging through coarse scrub did not seem so bad. Finally we saw far below us a stone cottage. As we approached it, four guards, with rifles slung on their shoulders came towards us smiling, and greeted us with raised clenched fists and shouts of '*¡Salud, camaradas!*'

We flung ourselves down on the ground to rest and were given tin mugs of coffee without milk or sugar and great hunks of grey, powdery bread, of which I was later to become heartily tired. The guards told us that we had arrived on time.

I went inside the cottage to return my mug and to chat with one of the guards, who immediately asked me if I had any tobacco. I offered him a cigarette and to my surprise he broke it, put the tobacco carefully into a leather pouch and proceeded to roll a very thin cigarette using about one third of the tobacco I had given him. He puffed with evident satisfaction. 'I like English tobacco,' he said. 'It's smoother (*más fino*) than Spanish tobacco.'

The inside walls of the building were covered with autographs of hundreds of volunteers who had made the same journey and we searched for blank spaces where we could add our names, our home towns and the date.

41

Before Battle
(Thoughts of a twenty-one-year-old)

I have a dread of dying but
I have no fear of death
and wonder what will fill my mind
when I draw my last breath.
When death's hand switches out my life
and draws the heavy blind
regret, I think, will be the thought
that flashes through my mind;
regret for all those things I have
not done, for lack of time –
so many songs I could have sung;
so many words to rhyme;
so many places to explore;
so many things to love –
the wild flowers growing at my feet,
the birds and clouds above;
so many causes to defend;
so many fights not won;
so many challenges to make
before my life is done.
And if I live a hundred years
I'll not be weary yet.
I am in love with life and I
shall die with much regret.

Chapter 4 : Arrivals in Spain
11-15 November 1937

The sun rose higher in the sky, warm and bright. We sat talking in groups on the grass patch on the valley side of the cottage. The soldiers had stopped wandering from group to group, talking in sign-language. Instead, they spoke among themselves or to those of us who understood Spanish.

With the French coach-ride fresh in my memory I was surprised to find that the vehicles that were to take us on were four open lorries. We saw and heard them when they were still some way off, raising clouds of dust as they rumbled up the rough track that led to the frontier-post.

The lorries pulled up and the drivers left their cabs and strolled over to the soldiers. They seemed in no hurry to load up and drive off with their human cargo. After they had chatted with some of the volunteers and scrounged cigarettes, we were at last told to climb aboard.

We had to hold tight to the sides of the lorry or to each other as we bumped down the track for a couple of hundred yards. Then we turned left along a fairly good road and were able to sit down and have our first real view of Spain. The land seemed well-cultivated. In the fields on each side of the road peasants were hard at work. They were mostly women and old men. As they heard the lorries, they looked up and, in answer to our shouts of *'¡Salud!'* and *'¡Viva la República!'* They raised their clenched fists in greeting. The young army drivers drove fast, but there was little traffic on the road, just an occasional farm cart drawn by mules or donkeys and a few people on foot.

For more than an hour we sat, cramped and stiff in the lorry, cold in spite of the sunshine, until we reached Figueras. We drove through the narrow streets and entered the barracks that overlook the town. It was an enormous fort built, I was told, during the war against Napoleon, which the Spaniards called the First War of Independence. (The Second War of Independence was the one we had gone to Spain to fight in.)

The barracks, a large part of which was underground, were bursting with people. There were hundreds of Internationals. Some were new arrivals like us; others were veterans who were waiting to rejoin their units. There were also many Spaniards – Basques and Asturians for the most part who, having seen the north of Spain overrun by the Fascists, had made their way to France and then returned to Republican Spain to continue the struggle. So overcrowded were the barracks that the few latrines just could not cope, so most soldiers climbed up the slope and did what was necessary in the open fields. Luckily we spent only two nights in the barracks.

In the gloomy, subterranean dining-hall I had my first taste of Spanish wartime food. The main meal of the day was served at 1.30pm and consisted of some kind of stew containing beans, rice, lentils or chickpeas. The few tiny cubes of meat were rubbery, and no-one asked what kind of meat it was. The chickpeas (*garbanzos*) were often hard and indigestible. A thick slice of bread, which went stale very quickly, was served with the stew, as was a tin mug of sour red wine. Dessert was a handful of hazelnuts or a few grapes.

Both mornings we received some elementary military training. From a Soviet officer we learned how to take cover and crawl on our bellies, how a section should advance in open-order and the principles of camouflage. There was not a lot of 'square-bashing', though we did do some drilling to get us used to the Spanish military commands. Most of these seemed long-winded: *'¡En su lugar descansen!'* (stand at ease), *'Cabeza variación a la izquierda... ¡hip!'* (left wheel). To make us march in step, the instructor would yell what sounded like 'Oo! Oh! Eh! Arrow!', which I later realised was *uno, dos, tres, cuatro*.

As we were confined to barracks, we had to make our own entertainment. Impromptu concerts were held in the dormitories, long, underground halls filled with plank beds covered with straw-filled ticks. On these occasions anyone who could play a musical instrument, be it flute, violin, mouth-organ or guitar, was in great demand to accompany the singing.

I quickly picked up the words and melodies of many revolutionary songs. Each nationality took pride in singing its own songs, *Bandiera Rossa* and *Inno di Garibaldi* from the Italians, *Kevin Barry, Off to Dublin in the Green* and *Connolly's Rebel Song* from the Irish, *La Jeune Garde* from the French, *Die Rote Fahne* and *Brüder, zur Sonne, zur Freiheit* from the Germans. We English had little to offer. *The Red Flag* does not sound at all revolutionary and, in any case, the Germans thought we were singing a Christmas carol. But everyone seemed pleased when we roared out *It's a Long Way to Tipperary, Pack up Your Troubles in Your Old Kit Bag* and *Oh, My Darling, Clementine.*

The Ballad of Harry Pollitt proved very popular after we had translated the words. In the song, Harry dies and, claiming to be a friend of Lady Astor, gets admitted to Heaven, where he unionises the angels and brings them out on strike.[13] Arraigned before the Holy Ghost he is found guilty of 'spreading disaffection among the Heavenly Host' and sentenced to spend eternity in Hell. Harry doesn't care and 'tucking his nightshirt round his knees' floats down, soon to become First People's Commissar for Soviet Hell.

It was in Figueras that I heard for the first time *Jarama Valley*. Sung to the melancholy tune of *Red River Valley*, the words were written by Alex McDade, of Glasgow, who had been killed at Brunete four months previously. His was a protest song against the 'powers that be', and no-one knows who wrote the revised version. Only the first three lines of the opening verse are his:

> *There's a valley in Spain called Jarama;*
> *It's a place that we all know so well.*
> *It was there that we gave of our manhood,*
> *And many of our brave comrades fell...*[14]

On display in a large reading-room were newspapers from all over the world. Here, under the watchful eyes of Marx, Engels, Lenin, Stalin, President Manuel Azaña and *La Pasionaria*,[15] whose portraits adorned the walls, one could read, write a letter home or play draughts and chess.

The day after we arrived in Figueras we were given our first pay as soldiers, six peactas a day from the date we had left

Paris.[16] At the official rate of exchange it did not seem too bad, but we soon found that the prices of most things were high. The exceptions were drinks and fruit. One peseta would buy a glass of brandy or as many oranges as one could carry.

* * * * *

The following morning, on 13th November, a fresh batch of volunteers arrived, weary after their tramp over the mountains. We wondered where on earth they would sleep that night, as there seemed to be no spare room anywhere. However, a rumour soon went round that we were to leave that very day for Albacete, where the International Brigades had their headquarters. For once, the rumour proved to be true.

By five o'clock we had been given a piece of bread, some rock-hard *chorizo* and a tin of corned beef and were lined up in fours on the parade ground. After a roll call we marched off to the railway station, about four hundred of us, trying to look as military as we could in our civilian clothes.

We boarded a train that was waiting in a siding and made ourselves as comfortable as possible on the hard wooden seats. There was no glass in any of the windows, and only a few had been boarded up with plywood. It was impossible to escape from the cold wind that blew through the carriage.

When the train pulled out of the station we expected it to pick up speed, but it went at a steady fifteen or twenty miles an hour. It was a bumpy ride.

'There aren't any wheels on this bloody coach,' yelled one wag.

'Yes there are,' answered another, 'but the goddam wheels are square.'

We laughed and joked, threw bits of paper and orange peel at one another, sang and shouted, like schoolboys on an outing.

The train eventually reached what must have been its top speed, but as this was only about twenty-five miles an hour it was still possible to shout greetings to farmers working in their fields, children playing in the dust in front of their houses and lorry-drivers travelling along the road that ran by the side of the railway track.

'¡Viva la República!' we yelled.

'¡Viva!' they replied, raising right hands in clenched fist salutes.

The train stopped frequently. Sometimes we would be waiting for nearly an hour in a tiny station. The platform was immediately filled with people begging for tobacco or soap, or selling oranges, fizzy lemonade, figs and grapes. There were others who came merely to enjoy the spectacle.

As the station-master pulled the cord to ring the bell for the train to leave the station at a snail's pace someone started singing *The Internationale* and the crowd on the platform joined in.

We stopped for about two hours in a marshalling yard on the outskirts of Barcelona. The window-blinds were drawn and it was dark inside the carriage. We had been warned before leaving that in the aftermath of the fighting between the members of the POUM (Partido Obrero de Unificación Marxista) and the government forces we might not be too popular in Barcelona and therefore must keep the blinds drawn while in the city. This surprised me, as six months had passed since the fighting, which the government referred to as a Trotskyist uprising and, in any case, I considered myself an anti-fascist and a defender of democracy.

There was only one blue electric light-bulb in each carriage. It gave just enough light to make one's way to the lavatory without stepping on those who were stretched out to sleep in the centre aisle. The darkness had its effect on us. The singing and talking stopped and most of us settled down to sleep, some on the hard seats, some on the floor and some smaller men even climbed on the luggage racks.

When I awoke we were passing through Tarragona and it was broad daylight. The train was still travelling at no more than thirty miles an hour. Every hour or so it stopped, sometimes in a station, other times in open country. The driver always gave three or four loud whistle-blasts before setting off to make sure that he did not leave behind any who had alighted to wash in the irrigation canals or to pick oranges.

The whole morning passed in this way. At one station an old woman climbed into the train selling newspapers with exciting titles, *Frente Rojo* and *Solidaridad Obrera*. I bought one and started chatting to a Spanish soldier.

When at last we reached Valencia, where we guessed we would have to change trains, we were glad to be able to stretch our stiff legs after sitting for so long. We stood on the platform awaiting instructions and cheered when told that, as the Albacete train was not due to leave for five hours, we would be allowed to leave the station.

I felt rather like a tourist as I walked through the streets of the city which was the seat of the Spanish Republican government. I strolled slowly, finding interest in all I saw – the military uniforms, the political posters on the walls, the red stars and hammer-and-sickle emblems on some buildings. It was all so different from the pictures of Valencia that I had been shown by my Spanish teacher in school.

In a barber's shop I had a shave for one peseta. Pushing through the screen of coloured beads and stepping out into the bright sunshine I felt better and found a bar a few doors away, where I sat down with a glass of muscatel.

Back at the station we were all given a meal of lukewarm bean stew and a paper bag containing bread and more *chorizo* for the journey. The train was packed and I was glad to have arrived early and found a seat. Late-comers had to sit on the floor. Larry, from Milwaukee, was small enough to climb onto the luggage rack. I hardly slept at all. There was a constant hubbub of voices. Veterans of earlier battles told tales to wide-eyed recruits, and two or three card schools seemed to carry on all night.

I stood up to stretch my legs and look out of the window. Dawn had broken and in the distance I could see a range of mountains half-hidden in the morning mist. We had left far behind the fertile land of the Valencian plain, the orange groves, the melon fields and the semi-tropical vegetation. Now the landscape had a more forbidding aspect. Tall pines were the only trees in sight, while the slopes of the hills looked like arid, sandy wastes broken only by clumps of coarse bushes and patches of dry grass. We saw few villages, though the train frequently stopped to allow trains going in the opposite direction to pass on the single track.

By now the conversation had died down. The packs of cards had been put away, and there was no more singing. Tired, cold, hungry and bored with one another's company, we gazed out of the windows at the monotonous landscape, chins in cupped hands, without speaking.

Finally, at about half-past nine on 15th November, the train, still chugging along at no more than thirty miles an hour, entered a long cutting. We felt the brakes being applied as the train came slowly to a halt at our destination, Albacete. Immediately our mood changed. There were crowds on the platform to welcome us and we could hear a military band playing. There were banners everywhere, and the flags of Spain, France, Britain, Ireland, the US and others I did not recognise fluttered overhead.

We clambered down to the platform and, headed by the band of the International Brigades, marched through the streets of Albacete, winking at and shouting greetings to the girls we saw, waving our hands to women and children who looked down at us from balconies, and trying to march in step and look as soldierly as possible.

The band led us into the courtyard of a large house that had been requisitioned by the military. We were given a breakfast of bread and the black, unsweetened liquid which everyone called coffee. I have no idea what it was made of; some kind of roasted cereal, no doubt. It was bitter, but at least it was hot and we welcomed it.

Then came the inevitable form-filling. I was asked all about myself and my background by a clerk seated at a tiny desk. When he asked me my trade or profession I said: 'Newspaper reporter'. He wrote down on the form *'obrero'* (worker).

'Periodista' is the Spanish for "reporter",' I said.

'Yes, comrade, but we put down *obrero* for everyone. Do you belong to any political party?'

'Labour League of Youth,' I answered. He wrote down *'anti-fascista'*. This time I did not comment, but I wondered why he bothered to ask the questions.

República Española

Número de la libreta _78279_

Brigadas Internacionales

CARNET MILITAR PARA

Apellidos *Jump*

Nombre *James*

LEER CON ATENCION

1) Se ruega a los camaradas que a cada cambio, su Unidad haga la inscripción correspondiente.
2) No se extienden duplicados de este Carnet.
3) Los portadores del Carnet no tienen derecho a hacer inscripciones.

— 1 —

First page of James Jump's International Brigade carnet.

I then joined the long queue to collect my uniform. There was no attempt to issue uniforms of the right size. As we walked past the counter, a bundle of clothes was pushed into our hands, after which we were taken to have a hot shower. This was a luxury we had not expected, and we revelled in it, squealing with delight as we all stood naked in the large shower-room and felt the hot water running through our hair, over our eyes, nostrils and mouth and down our bodies.

Then we went into the next room to put on our uniforms. Each bundle contained a khaki cotton shirt, khaki trousers, underclothing, woollen socks, a pair of boots and either an overcoat or a poncho. I was lucky to have a poncho, because the

Page two of James Jump's International Brigade carnet.

collar could be buttoned down and the whole garment could then be used as an extra blanket. I was lucky too insofar as, being of roughly standard size, the uniform fitted me reasonably well. Some men looked like characters out of a circus.

There was much swapping of garments. Finally, most ended up with clothes that more or less fitted them, but some still looked comical.

After a meal of the inevitable bean stew, we were split into groups according to our native languages. It was explained to us that there were five training bases in towns or villages near Albacete. The base for English-speakers was at Tarazona. The French-speakers were at Madrigueras, and there were also bases for German-speakers, Italians and Slavs.

We waited for hours, had another medical examination and were issued with identity documents. At last, bored and impatient, we saw two covered lorries drive up and the English-speaking volunteers, mainly British, Irish, Canadians and Americans, were told to climb aboard.

We drove along the Madrid-Valencia road in the direction of Madrid. At La Gineta we turned to the right down a dusty lane full of potholes. The vehicles raised clouds of dense, white dust which filled our ears and eyes and whitened our hair and faces.

One stretch of the road was so bad that the lorry-drivers left it and found a less bumpy track across open country. It was quite dark when we reached Tarazona where, after a meal of vegetable soup and some kind of meat served with cooked tomatoes, we were bedded down, wrapped in rough blankets on the bare floor. It was bitterly cold, but I was so tired that I slept soundly until the sunlight came through the unshuttered windows next morning.

Pasionaria
(written on hearing of the death of Dolores Ibárruri)

Well I knew
that one day this moment would arrive
but my heart could not accept it
and even now I cannot believe, Dolores,
that you are no longer with us.

I saw you first when I was fighting-young.
You came to see us in the firing-line.
We drank up your eloquence
and we memorised all you said.
You inspired us,
fired us with increased courage.
Fifty years later I met you again
and with sorrow and pain
in my heart, I saw you
frail and fragile
but still with fire in your words.

For me you were not just a beautiful woman;
you were more than that.
You were an accomplished politician but, more than that,
you were a devout communist but, more than that,
you were the embodied spirit of Spain,
immortal Spain.
Dolores, I cannot believe
that you are dead
and so, for you,
I shall not wear black
but your favourite colour –
red.

'Enfermera, eres muy guapa' (Nurse, you are very beautiful*) 'Mi mejor amigo es mi fusil'* (My best friend is my rifle).

Political meetings were arranged by the political commissars, who were always glad to find someone prepared to lead a discussion on some specific topic.

During the evening of my first day in the recruit company I was visited by an American lieutenant who questioned me about my knowledge of Spanish. He was from the personnel office. Four days later, on 20th November, I was informed that I had been posted as interpreter to the machine gun company, even though I had not finished my basic training. The reason given to me was that the company commander, a German named Herman Engert[17] who spoke English well, knew very little Spanish, while the political commissar, a Spaniard, knew no English at all.

The machine gun company had its headquarters in a rambling two-storey house on the Albacete road not far from the square. I reported to Lieutenant Engert and was allotted a space in one of the upstairs rooms – just enough space for my straw-filled mattress, for the building was very overcrowded. The nights were bitterly cold and every morning I got up chilled to the marrow. After a few nights I used to make sure that I went to bed with a bottle of brandy, rum or *anís (*anise liqueur), from which I would take a swig every time the cold woke me. It did not make me any warmer, but it made the nights less unpleasant.

* * * * *

As each of the units was half Spaniards and half foreigners, the language difficulties were sometimes hard to overcome. The Spaniards were mostly raw young recruits who had been called up for military service a few weeks earlier. The foreign volunteers were mostly new arrivals like me, but there were some veterans, some who had been wounded and had come to Tarazona on their way home or in transit to their combat units.

In theory the foreigners were all English-speakers, but in practice there were a number of small groups or individuals who spoke neither Spanish nor English. All Finns had been posted to

Canadian units, probably because the first Finns to go to Spain had been living in Canada. There was one Japanese volunteer. Australians, New Zealanders and South Africans went to British units; Cubans and Puerto Ricans joined the Americans.

My duties were not arduous. Once I had learnt the names, in Spanish and English, of the parts of a machine gun and a number of military expressions, I found it quite easy to interpret the training instructions. Much more difficult was interpreting at political meetings and discussions. I almost despaired the day I first tried to do consecutive interpreting, where the speaker pauses after every sentence to allow for translation. Then, listening to other interpreters, I discovered that they had the same problem and overcame it by paraphrasing any expression that they could not translate directly. I soon learned the knack of this and also lost my nervousness of standing up in front of more than a hundred men and talking in a language that was not my own.

I had to do the normal military training and soon I could take to pieces a Russian Maxim and re-assemble it. I also had plenty of practice at digging fox-holes, constructing machine gun nests, learning about cross-fire, covering fire, scissor-fire and how to use the weapon economically. The machine guns were 1918 models and were enormously heavy, with their cast-iron wheels and large shield of quarter-inch steel. It took one mule or five men to carry one Maxim.

Our daily programme (Sundays excepted) was:

5.30am Reveille
5.45am Physical training
6.15am Breakfast
8am Saluting the flag
8.30am Military training
12.30pm Lunch, followed by siesta
3pm-5pm Political meetings, language classes etc
6pm Supper
9pm Lights out.

We would often march in the half light of early morning to the firing-range down the road that led to Motilla del Palancar, singing:

We will Franco's ranks demolish;
The great Miaja leads us on.
For on our rifles depends our freedom.
¡No pasarán! ¡No pasarán![18]

Most of the time I was in Spain I was hungry. We had regular meals at the training camp, except when we went out on all-day manoeuvres. The cookhouse staff worked hard with the limited supplies they received, doing their best to produce appetising meals – and were sometimes successful. That we left clean plates was a tribute to our hunger rather than to the quality of food we were given. The meals never completely took away our hunger. They merely reduced it enough to make life bearable until the next meal.

When we filed into the dining-hall, the trestle-tables had already been laid – eight places to a table. There were eight hunks of bread and eight cans (old food tins with handles soldered onto them) of red wine. Luckily we were in a part of Spain, La Mancha, famous for its excellent wine. On the tables were also salt, pepper and bottles of vinegar and locally produced olive oil, thick and green.

After a morning of digging fox-holes, taking part in manoeuvres or simply marching to and from the firing-range, we were ravenously hungry. Many Spaniards would spread olive oil and vinegar on their bread, sprinkle salt and pepper on it and devour it as if it were the finest food in the world while waiting for the first course, usually a stew of beans, lentils or rice brought into the hall in large galvanised buckets. I seldom did this but, having a sweet tooth, I occasionally bought from an itinerant street-vendor a thick slice of bread that had been fried in olive oil and then sprinkled with sugar.

Bread was never rationed in La Mancha, a wheat-growing region, and it would have been easy to go to the bakery and buy a loaf but very few men ever did so as there were posters everywhere urging us not to waste bread. Occasionally, however, one could see a uniformed figure slinking along the street that led from the bakery and having all the appearance of being five months pregnant.

Guard duty came round every four or five nights. The places guarded included the base HQ, the hospital, the telephone exchange, a water reservoir, a strategic bridge and the road leading out of Tarazona. These last three were not popular posts, especially on the midnight-to-two, and the two-to-four turns. They were isolated places; one got cold and bored. The most popular posts were those inside Tarazona: the hospital, the telephone exchange and the HQ. There, people were continually coming and going; there was always someone to talk to or share a cigarette with.

* * * * *

Being an interpreter seemed to bring me many extra chores, for there was much that could be done only by someone who spoke both Spanish and English. People were always coming to me with requests.

'We're trying to arrange Spanish lessons for beginners. Will you be the instructor – two afternoons a week?'

'I'm looking for someone to collect subscriptions for Socorro Rojo Internacional (International Red Medical Aid). Will you do it in the machine gun company?'

'I've had this letter from a girl I met in Valencia and I can't understand it. Will you read it to me, and then write a reply for me? I'll tell you what to put.'

'The company commissar thinks we should have a wall-newspaper. Will you be editor, comrade? You're the only person in the company who is a newspaperman.'[19]

I undertook these and many other tasks and I found that my Spanish improved rapidly, and I enjoyed my work, though it had its nerve-shattering moments, like the day I was called on to interpret at a meeting of *activistas*.

The gathering had been arranged by the Cultural Comm-Ission, a Spanish Communist Party offshoot that concerned itself with education – political for the most part – of the troops. There were a number of interpreters present and this, in itself, made me apprehensive, for all the others seemed to be natives of Spanish-speaking parts of the US and they were completely bilingual.

One of these Spanish-Americans was sitting near me and, whenever I was stuck for a word and hesitated, he whispered it to me. One word that foxed me was the Spanish for 'self-sacrifice'. '*Abnegación*,' he whispered.

Later, when the meeting ended he came over and spoke to me. I thought he was going to criticise my efforts, which I thought pretty poor, but instead he said: 'Gee, I wish I could speak Spanish like you, with that lovely Castilian accent. I just can't manage to pronounce my c's and z's like the Spaniards do.'

One of the most enjoyable jobs I had was to interpret for the American singer Paul Robeson. After he had spoken to the assembled troops he sang a number of Negro spirituals and revolutionary songs, ending with *The Internationale*. He signed his autograph for me on the only scrap of paper I had in my pocket. Years later I met him in London, and we had a long chat about his visit to Spain, and to Tarazona in particular.

* * * * *

Shortly after I arrived in Spain the Spanish government increased our pay to ten pesetas a day, thus bringing it into line with the pay of Spanish soldiers. We spent most of our money on drinks (fifty céntimos for a large glass of Málaga or muscatel). There was no beer to be had; nor could one buy cigarettes. Cigarettes or tobacco were issued to us at irregular intervals as a free ration. They were sent to Spain by voluntary organisations in France, the US and other countries. Occasionally there would be an issue of Spanish Ideales, which the Spaniards called *mataquintos* (recruit-killers), but the ration usually consisted of one packet of French cigarettes (Gauloises or Atlantis) or American cigarettes (Camel, Lucky Strike or Raleigh). Sometimes we were given Bull Durham tobacco in little linen bags.

The only English cigarettes we had were those received in letters from our families or friends. Nobody smoked 'tailor-made' cigarettes. It was the normal practice, on receiving a ration of cigarettes, to extract the tobacco and then use this to roll very thin cigarettes. At first, before I gained the knack, I used to produce the most grotesquely malformed smokes. I was so ashamed of them that I would often slip up a side street where no one could witness my pathetic efforts. After a while I became quite adept, though I never learned to roll a cigarette with one hand, as Lieutenant Cipriano could.[20] But he had lost one arm in battle, and so had no choice.

I was not a heavy smoker and, when no cigarettes were available, I just did not smoke. Some men had a real craving. I remember one who, when he received a tobacco ration, would mix it with a handful of straw from his palliasse to make it last longer. In the front line I've seen men rolling and smoking cigarettes made of dried vine leaves and pine-needles. Years later, Frank Deegan of Liverpool told me how he tried many substitutes and found that the best was dried potato leaves – little realising at the time that the potato and the tobacco plant are closely related.[21]

Guard Duty outside Tarazona de la Mancha

On guard duty at night
I discover
that there are degrees of blackness.
There is deep blackness all around me.
Not a flicker of light comes
from the village up the hill.
The sky is black
but the ground is blacker still
and blackest of all
Is the screen of trees, upright and tall
beyond the broken wall.

Here, eyes are useless.
I stare at invisibility
and feel the black invisibility
staring back at me, trying to discover, maybe,
why I am standing here.
I am looking for what I hope never to see;
I am waiting for someone I hope never to meet.
I do not want to challenge an intruder.
I do not want to meet a fifth-columnist.
I do not want to fire the one cartridge
in my antique rifle.

Here, eyes are useless
But my ears catch a thousand subtle sounds –
my own breathing,
the gritty scrape underfoot as I change my posture,
the flap of invisible wings overhead,
and the rustle of dry grass at the lane's edge.

A warm wind wafts the trees and they whisper,
'Stay alert, soldier!
Do not let your concentration slip.
No enemy will approach
but some officer may,
hoping to catch you dozing at your post.'

Chapter 6 : Transferred to headquarters
Mid December 1937-13 February 1938

One evening, about a month after arriving in Tarazona, a runner came with an order for me to report to the training camp HQ. When I got there I was interviewed by two comrades who did not speak a word of Spanish. They decided that I did, and next day's orders stated that I had been posted to the HQ as a clerk-interpreter.

Here the hours were longer and we worked seven days a week, but we had a number of privileges denied to other soldiers. We had no guard duties; neither did we go out on training exercises which, with the coming of the very cold weather, were no longer pleasant. But the greatest privilege was that the HQ staff, and the company commanders and commissars, had a separate dining-room. All the foreigners using it paid one-tenth of their pay towards mess funds and with this money the cooks purchased many extras which helped to make the wartime meals more palatable.

There were eight of us in the training camp office under Al, the chief clerk, a bearded New Yorker who was a professional musician.[22] He had brought his violin to Spain and at the end of the day he would play for his own (and our) entertainment. He preferred the classics but would play any tune we requested. All we had to do was hum the melody and Al would quickly pick it up.

If Paddy O'Sullivan, a Dubliner and one of the company commanders, was about he would be sure to ask Al to play Irish folk-songs, especially *The Kerry Dance*. Paddy, whose eyes would mist over as he listened, was, unlike most of the Irish volunteers, not a former Irish Republican Army man. He was said to be an ex-soldier of the Irish Free State and had a very military bearing. He was always smartly dressed and had the reputation of being a strict disciplinarian, but he was popular with his men.

Working under Al's direction were three Canadians, a Welshman,[23] two Londoners and a Spaniard. The Canadians were George Edgar,[24] from Fort Fraser, British Columbia, who must have been well over fifty years of age, Germain Ouellette[25] from Quebec and a young man whose name I forget. He was from Alberta and had enlisted under an assumed name so as not to harm his brother, who was in the Canadian Mounted Police.[26]

The Englishmen were Cyril Sexton, a gardener from Croydon, and Dave Newman, who had been a clerk in the offices

James R Jump (back row, second from right) in Tarazona on 12th January 1938, with (from left) George Edgar, William Durston, Dave Newman, Cyril Sexton and José García and (from right) Bill Beeching and Germain Ouellette.

of Edmonton borough council. Dave almost lost his life before he even reached Spain. His party travelled from Paris to Marseilles and there embarked on the *Ciudad de Barcelona*, an old pleasure-steamer. When the vessel was a few miles from Barcelona she was torpedoed by a fascist submarine and sank almost immediately. Dave was lucky. He was picked up by a fishing-boat and taken ashore, where he nearly died of pneumonia.[27]

The Spaniard in the HQ office was José García Gómez, a Catalan who had been living in Algeria. When he returned to fight for the Republic he was drafted into the International Brigades. He spoke fluent French, but no English.

My main task was to type out the daily orders, which were published in two versions – English and Spanish. This was always a worrying task as Juan Ponce, the base commissar, was fond of dashing into the office at the last minute with alterations and deletions. We possessed no duplicating machine and therefore Dave and I had to type the ten copies in each language. We found that, by using very thin paper and banging the keys as hard as we could, we could do five copies at a time, although the bottom copy was barely legible.

Each day we had to announce in the daily orders the password and counter-password for the guards to use, and it was our job to select them from a dictionary. For a laugh José and I started to pick words with a double meaning, like *huevos* (eggs: balls) or *chorizo* (sausage: penis), or topical words. On one occasion the password was *generalísimo* and the counter-password *hijo de puta* (son of a whore). Our choice of words used to amuse the Spaniards and often it was the first item they read when the daily orders were pinned up.

I also had to be available at all times for general translating and interpreting. My work brought me into close contact with the base commandant, a tall bespectacled American named Allan Johnson.[28] I often wondered whether he ever despaired of turning the new recruits who reached Tarazona into disciplined soldiers. If he did, he never showed it. He was always cheerful and, though he insisted on strict discipline, I never heard him speak sharply to anyone. He disliked making speeches, and

65

always left that to the commissar. He was aware of the weaknesses of the Spanish army, and that is why he always impressed on those who passed through his hands the importance of what he called 'organisation of terrain'. He never ceased stressing the value of consolidating conquered ground, and one of his favourite pieces of advice was: 'The fascists are smart sons-of-bitches. Be prepared for their counter-attack.'

Major Johnson wrote a number of articles on this subject for *The Volunteer for Liberty*, the organ of the International Brigades, which was published weekly in English, French, German, Italian, Polish and possibly other languages as well.

The commissar, Juan Ponce, was a jolly little Spaniard who was happiest when helping someone to understand the intricacies of the Spanish language. I think he had been a teacher before the war. It was he who said to me, the day I joined the HQ staff: 'You speak very good pre-war Spanish, but we don't speak like that anymore. Do not call me *señor* but *camarada*, and address me as *tú* and not as *usted*.'

There was only one Russian in Tarazona, and we never knew his real name. He was known to everyone as Captain Ramón, and he spoke almost perfect Spanish. He was always to be seen on the training ground or the rifle range and he never spoke of anything except military matters. He left Tarazona early in 1938 and returned, I believe, to the Soviet Union.

The base postman was Taffy, a Welsh miner whose shoulder had been almost blown away by a soft-nosed bullet.[29] Daily he travelled to Albacete in the truck to bring back the mail. Needless to say, he was one of the most popular men in Tarazona. Even more popular, once every ten days at any rate, was the paymaster, Marcelino García.[30] Despite his name, Marcelino (or Marshall, as the Americans called him) was a US citizen and told me that he had emigrated as a child with his parents from Asturias to California. He used to claim that the Spanish Civil War was his fourth war, having fought in Flanders, Mexico and Cuba. Whether this was true or not, I wasn't sure, but when he was in a talkative mood he would take off his shirt to display the wounds he said he had received in those campaigns.

Marcelino gave me a piece of advice. 'Don't worry if you shit your pants the first time you go into action,' he said. 'It's natural to be shit-scared when some goddam sons-of-bitches are trying to shoot you. It's OK to feel scared but what you must never do is panic.'

* * * * *

A few days before Christmas I was on duty in the orderly-room at about half-past ten at night when the phone rang. It was someone ringing up from the headquarters of the Assault Guard in Tarazona.[31]

'Have you heard the news, comrade?'

'What news?'

'We've captured Teruel.'

'What?' I couldn't believe my ears.

'Yes, it's true. Teruel is in our hands. We have just heard the news on the radio.'

So I had the pleasure of telling Major Johnson that Teruel had been liberated by the Spanish People's Army. He blinked, put on his glasses and ordered me to take a bottle of brandy and two glasses from a cupboard so that we might toast the success. The news spread through Tarazona like wildfire and produced a state of euphoria. What would the Republic's next objective be – Saragossa? Every soldier became a military expert and worked out plans for the next offensive.

Christmas Day was a holiday and the news from Teruel certainly gave us something to celebrate. We had a ration of cigarettes and each British volunteer received a parcel from Charlotte Haldane's International Brigade fund,[32] and Americans and Canadians also received parcels from similar organisations in their countries. Each of our parcels contained tea, sugar, cocoa, chocolate, cigarettes, toothpaste, razor-blades, two Penguin novels and a Christmas card signed by Harry Pollitt.

In the dining-room, which was decorated with political slogans for the occasion, we had a special meal – soup, half an egg, boiled fowl with potatoes and stewed plums and custard. And a double ration of wine!

In the evening a party of us had supper with a Spanish family. We had given them the money and they provided us with roasted goat served with red peppers and tomatoes, fresh bread and wine. I sat next to the oldest member of the family who looked ninety but was probably not much over sixty. He asked me the question I so often heard in Tarazona: 'Are you an American from England or from America?'

'I'm from England.'

'I have a son who used to live abroad.'

'Oh yes? Where did he live?'

'In Bilbao.'

I found that most of the old folk had little knowledge of Britain or America, and to try to explain that a Scot is not an Englishman was to attempt the impossible.

After supper we returned along the dark streets to the HQ, where a sing-song was in progress. After a time the party became rather noisy and hectic, especially when Allan Johnson, who usually kept to himself, appeared with a bottle of cognac and two bottles of rum. Thus, we had one day's rest. On Boxing Day reveille sounded at 5.30am and life returned to normal, except that not a few men had hangovers. Yet there was no exceptionally large sick-parade. Men who reported sick for trivial matters were despised by their comrades and were always called 'goldbricks'; I don't know why.

In addition to my official duties, I was often asked to act as interpreter in private matters. One day Sergeant Lambert asked me for help. John Lambert was known by sight to everyone in the camp, as he had had made to measure a uniform of dark brown corduroy. He told me that he had fallen in love with a local girl. She was one of the cleaners who came to the *estado mayor* (HQ) every morning to sweep, dust and scrub. They wanted to marry and her parents had given consent, but there was one snag. The mayor of Tarazona had asked Lambert for a 'reference' and he hadn't got one. I went with the couple to see the mayor. Yes, said the mayor, before he could marry them he had to have a reference from Lambert's last employer. Spain must be sure that he did not have a criminal past.

Unfortunately Lambert's last employer was the British Army, and Lambert had deserted in order to fight in Spain, so it would be quite useless asking the War Office in London for a reference. There was no solution, so in the end the couple decided to live together as man and wife. For the sake of the girl's family and to prevent malicious gossip, they announced that the reference had been received and that they were going to be married in Albacete. Allan Johnson connived at this deceit by giving Lambert a leave pass. All the friends and relatives seemed to accept the story.

So, with the good wishes of everyone they left for Albacete on the bus which did one journey each way every day. Two days later they returned, both wearing wedding rings. From then on Lambert lived with his 'in-laws', though he spoke no more than half-a-dozen words of Spanish. I often wondered how they managed.

They were a lovely couple and very much in love. Johnny eventually returned to Britain but I do not know if he ever managed to get his 'wife' to join him. After the war it was almost impossible even for legal wives to escape from Franco's Spain.

* * * * *

After Christmas the weather turned bitterly cold and one morning we got up to find that it had snowed in the night. The dirt streets of Tarazona, dusty in dry weather and muddy when it rained, were frozen iron-hard. The old men who used to gather in the square every morning to gossip and enjoy the sunshine still met, but they had blankets round their shoulders and they stamped their feet to keep warm.

Early in January I received a home-made plum-pudding which my parents had sent me. The problem was how to eat it? At first we thought of cutting it into slices and toasting over the *brasero* (an iron tray filled with glowing charcoal, which was the only heating in the office). Then José García, who seemed fascinated by the pudding and was curious to sample it, had a brain-wave. He arranged with a Tarazona family to lay on a supper for us, the *pièce de résistance* of which would be the

69

Christmas pudding. We managed to obtain some *garbanzos* from the stores and each of us chipped in with a few pesetas, and we left it to the housewife to arrange the meal.

That evening we sat at a round table, in the centre of which was placed a large dish containing the stew – rabbit with *garbanzos* and potatoes and flavoured with saffron, garlic and onion. There were no plates. Each of us had a spoon in one hand and a hunk of bread in the other and dipped into the communal bowl. There were no glasses for the wine, but a *porrón* (glass decanter with a long spout) of *tinto* (red wine) circulated throughout the meal.

Under my direction the pudding had been heated. When it was turned out onto a plate all the family, from the white-haired grandmother to the youngest child eyed it with wonderment and even awe. We tried to get them to taste it, but none of the grown-ups dared to. The children, however, were more adventurous. They tried it, liked it and even asked for more.

About this time I joined the Spanish Communist Party. This was the 'in' thing, and a large number paid the annual subscription and received party cards. It was little more than a formality, as we had very few meetings and never seemed to have any close contact with the local Tarazona branch. Once or twice we were asked to attend a meeting of *activistas*, where we were exhorted to set the other soldiers an example in efficiency, enthusiasm and devotion to duty. Most volunteers also paid annual subscriptions to the Socorro Rojo Internacional and to the Amigos de la Unión Soviética.

Early in February Al, the chief clerk, left the Tarazona training camp HQ to join the Abraham Lincoln Battalion, and I was appointed in his place, but I was not chief clerk for more than two weeks.

British International Brigaders' Reunion

There are still about one hundred of us,
skin-furrowed and either bald or white,
and many are here today
with their wheelchairs,
walking-frames,
crutches
and walking sticks.
I am surrounded by trembling hands,
unsteady legs and cracked voices.

In 1937 there were few Brigaders younger than me
so it's quite on the cards that if I really try not to get ill
one day I may be
the last British volunteer alive.
I hope this happens;
what fun I'll have!
I shall tell tall tales
and no-one will be there to call me a liar.
I shall speak of my bravery under enemy fire
when I led the crossing of the Ebro
in the Republic's last offensive.
I shall mention how I advised the divisional commander
and how the minister of war himself
consulted me.
What a time I'll have!

But I was born under an unlucky star
and perhaps I shall not be the last to die.
Then, from above, I shall have to listen
to exaggerated tales told by some comrade of mine
and I, from up above,
shall not be able to call him a liar.

Chapter 7 : I acquire a status symbol
14 February-15 March 1938

For some days there had been a rumour that a lot of men were to be posted to combat units. The Tarazona training camp was certainly very overcrowded. New recruits kept arriving, and at the morning flag-raising parade the square was packed with men. When Major Allan Johnson sent for me on the evening of 14th February I assumed that he would inform me that I was to join the British Battalion at the front.

'Can you add up and subtract, comrade?' he asked.

Somewhat taken aback by the question, I said that I believed I could.

'Good!' he replied. 'I'm going to make you paymaster.'

'What? Me! Paymaster?' I stammered.

'Yes. Marshall García has been pestering me for a long time to send him to join the Lincolns, and a draft is due to leave very soon. I told him I couldn't let him go until I found a replacement. It has to be someone who speaks both languages and can look after the books, and you'll do.'

I hurried through the dark streets, slipping over the frozen earth to the main square where Marshall, or Marcelino as I called him, had his office in a converted shop. He was already packing his belongings.

Marcelino handed me the keys of the safe and told me how to change the combination to any four-letter word I wished. 'And I know which four-letter word you'll pick,' he said with a mischievous grin, digging me in the ribs.

He allowed me to check the books and see that the cash balance in the safe was correct. Then he sold me a pair of brown shoes for ten pesetas and presented me with a Spanish-English dictionary. 'That's it,' he said, taking up a bottle of rum that he had removed from the safe. 'Now you can drink to my good luck.'

So I became camp paymaster. The appointment appeared in the next day's orders, and Allan Johnson gave me an authorisation to draw from the armoury the pistol and twenty-five rounds of ammunition that García had handed in.

'I hope you never have to use the goddam thing,' he said, 'but I've got to cover myself. You are in charge of a hell of a lot of dough. If anything happens to it, I shan't be blamed provided you are armed.'

The author in Spain in late 1937 or early 1938.

I strolled down the hill to the armoury where I was handed a Belgian Le Page 7.65mm automatic, which the armourer showed me how to strip, clean and load. The same day the draft left for the front, and Tarazona was almost empty of troops. Only the newest recruits and the administrative staff remained.

My 'promotion' to paymaster did not give me any increase in pay or any stripes. Real promotion had to be made in the front line, and any other promotion was temporary and unpaid. Juan Ponce, the political commissar, who had gone with Marcelino

García's draft, had reverted to private. But, though I had no promotion, I did have a status symbol – my pistol, in a leather holster hanging from my belt. As most pistol-holders were officers, I was often saluted, especially by recruits.

Early in 1938 the Spanish government had issued a number of orders designed to improve the discipline of the army. One of these concerned saluting. Articles in *The Volunteer for Liberty* told us that a salute was a soldier's way of saying 'hello' and that all officers should be saluted. This was never really accepted by International Brigaders. We were prepared to salute the flag of the Republic and to salute officers when we were on duty. Off duty, however, we continued to use their first names. We felt that this, and the complete absence of spit-and-polish and other 'bull', were the outward and visible signs of the fundamentally democratic nature of the International Brigades, in which there was no blind obedience to orders. Troops had the right to discuss orders and to criticise commands. In practice, it seemed to work, for I cannot recall ever receiving an order that we felt was unreasonable (and I cannot say the same of some orders I received in the British Army during the Second World War).

The real advantage of being paymaster was that I had my own office, the shop on the plaza facing the church. At the rear of the shop was a large room containing the safe, a telephone, a table and two chairs, a cupboard, a sink with running water and a bed. This was the greatest luxury. I could sleep in a bed again – for the first time since leaving Béziers in November. A 'char' was employed to come in daily to clean the place.

I was, indeed, my own master, though I was obliged to stay in the office most of the time. I was answerable only to Major Johnson and the political commissar, an American called Howard Goddard. They very seldom took any interest in what I did, providing things ran smoothly.

Every ten days I had to collect the company commanders' lists of personnel on their strength. It was my job to add them up and then, a day or two before pay day, travel to Albacete in the staff car, an old Ford driven by an even older American from Wisconsin. There I collected from the Banco de España enough money to pay the troops (sometimes nearly one hundred thousand pesetas). Then, on my return, the money was distributed among the units. Members of the HQ staff, from Major Johnson and the political commissar down to the cooks, clerks and runners, came to my office to draw their pay.

* * * * *

There was always a shortage of small change in Tarazona, especially on payday. With the pay of Brigaders having been increased to ten pesetas a day, we were paid every ten days and this, in itself, presented a problem. Five hundred men, each with a 100-peseta note, would be wandering round Tarazona looking for a bar where they could buy a one-peseta glass of brandy or a glass of wine for fifty céntimos. There was just not enough change in circulation. This was partly overcome by an order of the government allowing town councils to print 'local' money. Thus there were one-peseta notes issued by the Tarazona council, but their value was nil outside Tarazona. Shopkeepers would accept notes issued in Madrigueras or other villages nearby, but notes from places further afield were valueless.

In addition, at my suggestion, Allan Johnson authorised the printing of cardboard counters representing small change. On one side of the counter, which was about the size of a twopenny-piece, was printed the coat of arms of the Republic and on the other was affixed a postage stamp, the value of which indicated the value of the counter. Also printed on the counter were the words 'For use only in the canteen'.

Local tradespeople, however, not wishing to lose business and having confidence in the solvency of the International Brigades, started accepting them as legal tender and within a few days the counters were in general use. Consequently, bar and shopkeepers every day and market stall-holders once a week would come to my office with pockets stuffed with counters for me to change into Bank of Spain notes.

I was also responsible for paying local tradespeople – carpenters, plumbers etc – who had to be called in to do repairs. It would have been simple to embezzle money if I had wished to. Many Spanish recruits and most of the Tarazona tradesmen were illiterate. I always kept an ink-pad on my desk so that I could obtain thumb-prints in lieu of signatures on receipts.

I remember one mistake I made. A carpenter called at the office with a bill for four pesetas and fifty céntimos (4.50 pesetas). The decimal point (a comma in Spain) must have not been clearly written, or I was daydreaming, for I gave him a 500-peseta note and asked him if he had fifty pesetas change.

'*Hombre*, it's not that much!' he said. 'If you give me five pesetas, I'll give you two *reales*.'

To the right of my office was a bank. On the left was a narrow alley leading to the guard room, and beyond that was a drapers. On the side of the square to the left of my office was the headquarters of the Guardia de Asalto y Seguridad (Assault Guard). On the other side were the telephone exchange and a stationer's. The exchange was run by a Valencian named Ortiz, whose son, a lad of about seven, often used to come and talk to me. There were not many phones in Tarazona and when one rang up (by turning the handle by the side of the phone) it was often the seven-year-old who answered: '*¡Dígame!* What number do you want?'

There was a cinema in Tarazona where films were shown once or twice a week. The Spaniards used to pack the place but few Internationals went, as the old films were either Spanish-made or dubbed with Spanish speech. Occasionally a good film was shown, like *Battleship Potemkin*, but usually they were poor quality; I remember seeing *Mercedes*, a romantic film which had been popular in Spain for some years, mainly because of the song duet:

Mercedes, mi vida entera es para ti.
Roberto, sin ti no puedo yo vivir.
(Mercedes, my whole life is yours.
Roberto, without you I cannot live.)

The weekly market in the plaza offered little of good quality except fruit, which was dirt cheap. For the rest, one could buy cheap jewellery, fans (made in Japan), poor quality cotton socks that lost their shape after one wash, old numbers of magazines and political badges. There was always a wide range of red stars, hammer-and-sickle brooches and pins, and enamelled badges bearing the head of Lenin. There was no personality cult of any Spanish politician. The two most popular Spaniards at that time were General José Miaja, 'the defender of Madrid', and the communist minister and powerful speaker Dolores Ibárruri, known as *La Pasionaria*.

Many men used to adorn their uniforms with political badges. The insignia of the International Brigades was a three-pointed red star worn on the cap or beret. Many Spaniards chose to wear red ties or neckerchiefs showing that they were either socialists or communists. A few wore black and red neckerchiefs, denoting that they were anarchists.

Often, when I went to Albacete I would spend the night there, sleeping in a hostel for servicemen run by the Socorro Rojo Internacional. This enabled me to visit the cinema or the theatre. The theatres mostly had revues or variety shows and the turns were often singers who sang patriotic or revolutionary songs. The audience was usually composed largely of servicemen. There was also a bookshop. On one occasion I purchased *De un momento a otro* by Rafael Alberti.

I was the only person legally entitled to change foreign money and occasionally a few francs, dollars or shillings came into my safe where they remained until I next went to Albacete, when they were changed in the Banco de España. Some volunteers brought me valuables to be locked in the safe until they wanted them again.

I had to keep a record of all financial transactions ranging from canteen profits, in the region of two thousand pesetas a month, to a five-peseta fine for drunkenness. Besides the books of the canteen, I had to audit the accounts of the commissariat and the quartermaster's stores once a month. Major Johnson used to check my books once every month or six weeks.

A few weeks after becoming paymaster I persuaded him that I really ought to have an assistant. He looked at me quizzically, and I hastened to explain. 'There's a lot more work since we introduced the canteen tokens and, as the shopkeepers use them, it hardly seems fair to close the office for long periods when they want to cash them.'

Johnson did not say anything, so I went on: 'If I had an assistant, there will be no problems when my time comes to join the British Battalion.' This seemed to convince him and he told me that, if I knew anyone who would do, I should let him know. I immediately suggested Bill Harrington, from Stoke Newington, who had arrived in Tarazona a few weeks previously.

'I see you have it all worked out, you scheming son-of-a-bitch,' he said with a smile.

Harrington, at the age of twenty-five, had served in and been kicked out of the RAF, worked as a pilot for a Portuguese East African airline, when one of his jobs was to fly out from Addis Ababa to Djibouti the staff of Haile Selassie when Ethiopia was invaded by the Italians. After that, he told me, he had flown planes to Republican Spain in contravention of the League of Nations' Non-Intervention Committee until he found that the British police were after him. He then tried to join the Spanish Air Force but found that it was barred to foreigners, so he joined the International Brigades. Bill fancied himself as a poet and some of his verses were published in *The Volunteer for Liberty*.[33]

The pleasant life of paymaster could not last forever. Allan Johnson told me that he intended posting me to the training school for NCOs as soon as Bill Harrington could take over from me. But before he could carry out his intention, my phone rang again and I was told to report next day, 16th March, to the headquarters of the International Brigades on the Plaza del Altozano, Albacete, where I was to be employed as a clerk-interpreter. Bill Harrington took over from me and, next morning, I left Tarazona for the last time.

No-Man's Land

There comes a lull –
a pause in the firing of guns and,
with unhurried wings,
a large black bird
takes advantage of the quiet interlude
to fly over no-man's land
to safety behind our lines.

The trees, burnt and headless
are but blackened stumps.
The grasses and weeds that once blanketed their roots
are charred and dead.
This is more than no-man's land, I think
It is a dead land.
It is a no-life land.
But I am mistaken.
A nervous, inquisitive ant
explores the back of my grimy hand
and I wonder, 'How can such a weak and tiny creature
survive in no-man's land?'

Chapter 8 : Bad news from the front
16 March-7 April 1938

I had been instructed to report to Lieutenant Alec Cummings, who was in charge of the British section of the International Brigades' *servicio de personal* (personnel office) in Albacete. He was a tall, good-looking man with blue eyes and curly straw-coloured hair. He explained to me that the *servicio de personal* had recently been reorganised. Previously there had been one office dealing with all English-speaking volunteers. 'The organisation seems too big, too complicated,' he said, 'so it has been split into smaller units – one branch for the Americans, one for the British and one for the Canadians. I think it will function more efficiently.'

Cummings introduced me to a Spaniard named Vicente Gregorio Terol, who handled the records of all Spaniards serving with the British Battalion. Terol seemed happy to have someone with whom he could converse in Spanish, but Cummings called me back to his room.

'The first thing we must do is apply for permission for you to work here.'

'I thought it was all arranged,' I said. 'Major Johnson told me I had been posted here.'

'That's right, comrade, but normally no-one is allowed to hold a desk job at headquarters until he has served at the front for at least two months. I shall have to write to the director-general of the International Brigades to make an exception in your case.'

My first task, therefore, on 16th March, was to type out a letter requesting permission for me to be employed in the personnel office until a replacement with the necessary qualifications could be found. The letter was signed and sent by special messenger and, within an hour, permission had been granted.

Cummings then told Vicente to show me where I would sleep. It was a large building by the side of one of the roads that led into the Plaza del Altozano and this served as a dormitory for all the soldiers working in the International Brigades' head-quarters. I left my blanket and haversack there and strolled back to the office.

Next I went, armed with the reply from the director-general, to the security office where I was given two identity cards, one to admit me to the personnel office and the other to allow me to use the dining-room where all the HQ staff ate. This was a converted office on the Plaza del Altozano. Only when these formalities were completed could I settle down to work and take stock of my surroundings.

The British section of the *servicio de personal* was on the first floor of an office building which, before the war, had housed the Albacete chamber of commerce. On the door one could still see the brass plate inscribed 'Círculo Mercantil de Albacete'. On the opposite side of the square were a number of shops; on the left was the Capitol Theatre.

I went to the theatre as often as I could while I was stationed in Albacete. Apart from it being a pleasant way to spend an evening, it was a painless way of improving my Spanish. Very few plays were performed while I was there. For the most part I saw variety shows and revues. There was never any crooning à la Bing Crosby, which was so much the craze in Britain at that time; nor was there any tap-dancing à la Fred Astaire. Most of the artists sang flamenco or danced *habaneras*, *jotas* or *seguiriyas*. Women in pseudo-military attire sometimes sang patriotic songs that had the tempo of a *pasodoble*. There were no slapstick comics nor any of those comedians who just come on the stage and tell a string of jokes, though occasionally an artist would sing a satirical ditty about Franco, Mussolini and Hitler. The sentimental dramatic monologue, still heard in the thirties in English variety theatres, had no place in these Spanish programmes, but the poems of Federico García Lorca were often recited, and thunderously applauded.

At first, I was fascinated by flamenco, though I did not understand it and could not say with honesty that I liked it, but eventually my ears became attuned to its rhythm and cadences until I was able at least to tell a good flamenco singer from a bad one.

Outside the office I did not have much to do with Vicente Terol. He was older than me, and right from the start he struck me as someone whose aim in life was to be an *enchufado*,[34] to have a safe cushy job as far away from any fighting as possible. He was also an inveterate scrounger. I worked in the same room as Cummings, and whenever he left the office, Vicente, who had a separate room, would be certain to knock at the door, which would then open just enough for his pale, pock-marked face to appear, and he would whine: *'¿Tienes un cigarillo por favor, camarada?'* (Have you got a cigarette please, comrade?)

I didn't mind sharing my cigarettes with him. After all, my parents used to send me ten Woodbines twice or three times a week folded in a copy of the *News Chronicle* or the local newspaper, whereas he only had the ration he was given. But I noticed that he frequently acquired chocolate, which he always munched in his little office without offering me any.

Terol spoke no English, so, whenever Cummings wanted to speak to him, I had to interpret. Our office hours had to fit in with the normal Albacete working hours. We did four hours in the morning, from 8am to noon, and then three hours in the evening from 4pm to 7pm. The weather was warm, and during the hottest hours of the day the whole city seemed to close down. Even the innumerable juvenile boot-blacks, newspaper vendors and the itinerant sellers of crucifixes and hammer-and-sickle badges disappeared from the streets.

There was one bookshop in Albacete where I often spent an hour or two browsing. Most of the shelves were devoted to political books – booklets containing the texts of speeches by President Manuel Azaña, Dolores Ibárruri and other politicians, or Spanish translations of Marx, Engels, Lenin and Stalin published in Moscow. There, however, always a good selection of poetry. Many of the poets were unknown to me at the time, but there were always copies of García Lorca's *Romancero gitano* in very cheap editions. The classics were hardly represented. It was easier to obtain a Spanish translation of *Great Expectations* than *Don Quijote* – even here in Don Quijote country.

It was pleasant to sit on a warm spring evening on one of the benches in the Plaza del Altozano. Loudspeakers in the trees relayed Spanish folk-songs and military marches, and there was never enough traffic to spoil one's enjoyment of the music, interrupted every hour or so by the news. Groups of children played games on the paths. The little girls played hopscotch or skipped, singing all the time in shrill voices. The favourite game of the boys was playing at soldiers, but occasionally a girl or two would be 'recruited'. They marched up and down, stamping their feet in time with the music from the loudspeakers. They had sticks which served as rifles and one of the oldest in the group drilled them, just as we had been drilled, shouting out the long-winded Spanish commands: *'¡En su lugar descansen!'* (Stand at ease) *'¡Firmes!'* (Attention) *'¡Presenten armas... hip!'* There always seemed to be a toddler at the end of the column who fell over and burst into tears or who had to be reprimanded for his slowness. It was just like our training.

* * * * *

The work was interesting. I had to maintain a card-index of all the British soldiers in the International Brigades, so that any man could be contacted without undue delay. This was far from easy, as they were constantly being posted from one unit to another or entering or leaving hospital. Many Britons were attached to other units of the Spanish People's Army. New cards had to be prepared for the recruits who arrived every few days in Figueras.

There was a 'dead' file, a separate index, where we kept the cards of all men killed in action, together with those who were known to be prisoners of war, those who had been repatriated and the few, very few, who deserted.[35] The accuracy and up-to-dateness of this index was essential if we were to do our job efficiently. Urgent requests for the names of two men who could drive and service lorries, or a man who could speak French, would send me searching through the cards.

Once a week a bundle of letters and parcels came from the International Brigades' post office to be readdressed and forwarded. Finally, there was the general correspondence, which occupied most of my time. Much of this came from the British consul, acting on behalf of worried parents whose sons had not written home for a long time. Occasionally I would have to write stating that the man was dead or missing; more often I wrote to the man asking him to write to his family.

I used to write many letters to parents and Members of Parliament who alleged that their sons or constituents had been tricked into going to Spain by offers of large sums of money. I found that the best way to deal with such ridiculous complaints was to get the volunteer himself to write home giving his real reason for volunteering – his political convictions.

I remember the correspondence we had about George X.[36] His father, a Church of Scotland minister, wrote to his MP alleging that George had been enticed to Spain by scoundrels when he was only twenty years of age. The MP had written to the consul asking him to procure the young man's return to Scotland.

We wrote to George, explaining the whole position and asking him if he wished to go home. A week later the reply was received. He admitted telling a lie about his age when he volunteered, but added that he was now twenty-one, and preferred to stay in Spain while the job he had come to do remained unfinished. I doubt if George's father believed the reply. I hoped that George would come through unscathed and return home to argue it out with his reverend father.

Another day we had to interview a young Portuguese man who had deserted from the fascist army and surrendered to a unit of the British Battalion. Though we spoke no Portuguese, Vicente and I discovered that we could understand him reasonably well. I gave him a cigarette and he was happy to tell me his story.

At the time of the outbreak of the Spanish Civil War, he had been arrested for left-wing activities at Coimbra University. For eight months he was kept in prison, without a trial, until he and all the other prisoners, political and criminal, were told that they would be released and pardoned if they would volunteer to join Franco's Foreign Legion. He was one of hundreds who accepted this offer, but from the beginning he had decided that, at the first opportunity, he would desert and offer his services to the Republic. He had come to fight for the Republic, he said. 'I'm a socialist and am happy to be here with comrades,' he concluded.

I told Lieutenant Cummings his story, and he asked me: 'What do you think?'

'It sounds genuine,' I replied, 'at any rate, the way he tells it.'

'We'll give him a chance, then. After all, how much do we know of the political background of many of the volunteers who come from England? One more gamble won't make any great difference.'

So the Portuguese student was given a good meal and his military police escort was dismissed. I made out an index card for him and saw him driven off to Tarazona on a lorry.

* * * * *

For some time before I moved to the personnel office the news from the Teruel front had been getting daily more ominous. At first the confidence that our offensive had inspired in us remained, and we shrugged off reports of massive Fascist counter-attacks saying, in the words of Major Allan Johnson: 'They're clever sons-of-bitches, these fascists! Let's hope our troops have organised their terrain effectively.'

It became clear, however, that things were not going well. Franco had been able to bring up reinforcements, including thousands of Italian and Moorish troops, and his planes – Capronis, Messerschmitts and Heinkels – were almost unopposed in the air. The poorly equipped and ill-clad loyalist troops had 'dug in' in the snow-covered mountains but on 22nd February, Teruel was retaken by the fascists.

The propaganda machine of the Republic told us that this had been a victory, as it had taken Franco two months to take back what the Republic had won in a few days, but I don't think many people were fooled. The official war bulletins referred daily to 'stubborn resistance' and 'withdrawal to prepared positions', but we could read between the lines. Our forces were in retreat. This was confirmed by the reports I read in the newspapers which my parents regularly sent me.

85

At last the government was forced to tell the people just how grave the situation was. The Juventudes Socialistas Unificadas (United Socialist Youth), composed of socialists and communists, called for the formation of a youth division and carried out propaganda to achieve this end. Meetings and demonstrations were organised in Albacete and on 27th March I saw hundreds of volunteers, all in their teens, marching to the railway station.

We read the war communiqués every morning, wondering where the fascist advance would be halted. Each day the enemy salient stretched nearer and nearer to the Mediterranean. If they reached the sea, the Republic would be cut in two. Early in April, fascist radio announced that Lérida had been captured and there were rumours that Tortosa had fallen. The prime minister of the Republic, Dr Juan Negrín, reorganised the cabinet and took charge of defence.

Then, on 6th April, Alec Cummings returned from a meeting with startling news. 'The headquarters of all the International Brigades are to be transferred to Barcelona.'

'Why?' we asked him.

'Nearly all the Internationals are fighting in the north, and in the event of the fascist forces reaching the Mediterranean they must not be cut off from their base. It would be impossible for us to do our work in such circumstances.'

'When do we leave?' I asked.

'I've no idea, but we must be ready to take the train some time tomorrow. We must take with us all our records and office equipment. Any unimportant documents must be destroyed. We also ought to burn any correspondence which, in enemy hands, might incriminate 'friendly' politicians in any neutral country. After all, our train might be derailed or captured by the fascists.'

All that day and all through the night Lieutenant Cummings, Vicente Terol and I worked, with only short breaks for meals and drinks. By half-past six next morning our once tidy offices were littered with torn paper and bits of string. Cardboard and wooden boxes containing all we proposed to take with us were stacked in one room. In the other were boxes of things that could not be taken. They included thousands of cigarettes, boxes of milk chocolate bars and cartons of soap that had arrived only two days previously from the London Committee for Spanish Relief.

'What's going to happen to all that?' I asked.

'I don't know,' answered Cummings. 'I'll find out after breakfast. We may not be able to take it with us.'

We went to the staff restaurant for coffee and bread and soon after returning to the office the telephone rang and Cummings answered it.

'We're leaving some time today,' he said.

'And all this stuff?' I asked, pointing to the cartons of soap and cigarettes.

'My orders are that you may take as much as you can carry. The rest we shall give away to the locals. But first we must burn all the documents we are not taking with us.'

We worked all day packing and carrying downstairs sack-loads of old correspondence and documents which we put on a huge bonfire that blazed in the centre of the courtyard. We found cases of cigarettes, soap, toothpaste, knitted gloves and balaclavas and chocolate in a large cupboard that I had never seen before.

'We shan't have room for all that,' said Cummings. 'Take what you want and give the rest away.'

Outside, the news spread like a grassland fire that we were giving away things that, to Spaniards in wartime, were more valuable than money. An enormous crowd gathered. We could not go down into the courtyard or we would have been mobbed by the people waiting to seize the articles we carried. We stood on the balcony, Terol and I, and threw down armload after armload of these luxury items. Women stood holding out their black aprons to catch packets of cigarettes, toothbrushes, chocolate, razor-blades and packets of sweets.

When it was clear that there was nothing left, the crowd dispersed. We sat down on the boxes and waited. We munched chocolate and sucked peppermints. For the first time in months we enjoyed the luxury of smoking whole cigarettes, not thin 'roll-ups'.

Thoughts on Immortality

It wouldn't happen to me, I thought.
It was something
that happened to other people –
the fellow we played cards with last night,
as like as not,
or even the lorry-driver who brought us, three days ago,
to this arid, out-of-the-way spot.

It couldn't happen to me, I reassured myself,
the fingers of hope squeezing out my fears
like paste from a tube.
After a few days
hiding from bullets
already past and spent,
hope turned to conviction
and I knew it wouldn't happen to me.

It hasn't happened to me, I reminded myself
as we queued for freedom,
discharge papers in hand.
I dismissed from my mind
all those poor comrades
whose discharge had been
bloody, premature and painful.

It never happened to me, I still say
years later, to anyone who has the time to listen.
Brave? Me? Not a bit of it!
I just kept my head down and kept my nose clean.

I still think it won't happen to me.
And if it does,
I shan't be around to know.

Chapter 9 : Escape to the north
7-13 April 1938

It was after two in the afternoon on 7th April when we were ordered to take the files, typewriters and boxes of documents down to the street and load them onto a lorry. That done, we climbed aboard, and were driven the few hundred yards to Albacete's railway station. There, we transferred everything to a luggage van, after which we collected a ration of bread and corned beef and were told to board the train.

There were no carriages, just goods wagons, and most of them seemed filled with soldiers. Vicente Terol and I were walking along the platform, wondering which van to climb into, when I heard someone shouting my name. I looked round and there, in one of the trucks, was José García, with whom I had worked in the Tarazona HQ. We turned back.

'Is there room for two in there?' I asked.

'Yes, comrade, come and join us.'

He offered me his hand and I scrambled into the wagon, followed by Terol. In the gloomy interior I saw more than a dozen men. Some were lying on their blankets; others were sitting with their backs against the sides of the wagon. We placed our belongings on the floor near where García had his things.

The train pulled out of Albacete shortly after half-past six and chugged down the single track in the direction of Valencia. None of us having slept the night before, we were dog-tired and glad to settle down for the night. There was, however, a snag. In order to breathe fresh air it was essential to leave one of the big sliding doors slightly open. This meant that some men were in a draught. As the air was warm nobody complained at first, but soon after darkness fell, an English voice shouted: 'Close the bloody door. I'm freezing.'

'Yes. Shut the goddam thing,' came an American voice. 'I'm as cold as a polar bear's ass.'

Those in the more sheltered part of the wagon protested, and a long argument followed. Finally we moved our things and all crowded together out of the draught. Now, I thought, I can get some sleep. But, as the night advanced it became colder in the wagon and, in turn, most of us were obliged to get up and empty our bladders. There was no lavatory, so we just had to do what was necessary standing up by the open door.

'Don't use the lavatory while the train is standing in a station,' yelled one joker.

In spite of the frequent disturbances and shouts whenever someone stumbled over a sleeping comrade or trod on his feet, I did manage to get a few hours' sleep, although the floor was hard and I suspected that the wagon had no springs.

When I finally awoke, we were approaching Valencia. The sun was shining brightly. I went and sat in the open doorway, my legs dangling, and looked at the scenery. The train was travelling so slowly that I had enough time to identify the trees growing in formation in the fields. I was struck by the great number of artesian wells, where I could see mules and donkeys walking slowly round and round, drawing up the water which flowed into the maze of irrigation ditches. I recalled Blasco Ibáñez's novel *La Barraca*, which I had read about a year previously, and I wondered who had first sunk these wells. Was it the Romans or the Arabs?

Around half-past eight the train came to a halt in a tiny station near a village called Alfafar – about five miles from Valencia. By now, most of my comrades were awake. We waited for the train to move again, but half an hour passed and there was still no sign of activity on the part of the engine-driver. One or two of us jumped down onto the track and I walked up to the driver's cab.

'How long are we going to be here, comrade?' I asked him.

He shrugged his shoulders. *'¿Quién sabe?'* he said. 'Who knows? But don't worry, I'll blow the whistle to give you time to get aboard before we leave.'

When this news was passed round there was a rush to get out of the wagons. We lay in the sun on the grass by the side of the track. José and I washed in one of the irrigation canals, after which we strolled along the track. The train was on a loop-line and we guessed that we were waiting for another train to go by in the opposite direction. We climbed onto the platform of the tiny station.

A little girl in a faded pink dress came up and offered us some oranges. She was barefoot. We each took some and gave her a few pesetas. She immediately started talking, but I could not understand a word of what she said.

'She's talking *valenciano*,' said José. 'It's a dialect of Catalan.' For a while he chatted to her, for Catalan was his native language.

* * * * *

The train remained on the loop-line all day and all the village turned out to meet us. At dinner time we were given a ration of one packet of tobacco each, so the old men of the village were even keener to come and talk to us. The villagers brought us fruit and wine; we gave them chocolate. In the late afternoon an impromptu concert was held on the station platform.

At dusk we were ordered back into the train but hardly had we settled down in our wagons than we were roused by shouts.

'*¡Aviación!*'

We descended and stood by the side of the train. In the direction of Valencia we saw searchlights probing the sky. Then we heard the booming of exploding bombs and the staccato thump-thump-thump of anti-aircraft fire. The raid lasted less than half an hour, after which there was absolute silence. One after one the searchlights faded, and we returned to our blankets.

I awoke to find we were travelling slowly by the side of the Mediterranean and, after we had passed through four or five stations, a Spaniard told me that we were only about twenty miles beyond Valencia. The train stopped at a tiny station, and suddenly the war came very close.

Most of the station buildings had been completely destroyed. They were just charred beams and heaps of rubble. On one of the tracks were the remains of a munitions train. All around we saw empty cartridge and shell cases. The thought that our train might become a target for the fascist bombing-planes was a sobering one and it affected us all. Our conversation suddenly became more subdued. Only after we had left the station did we start laughing and joking again.

We continued up the coast, passing through Castellón de la Plana and eventually turned inland, leaving the blue waters of the Mediterranean behind us. We passed the wreckage of another train and finally stopped at Alcalá de Chivert.

No sooner had we settled down to sleep than there was another air-raid warning. We were awakened by the cry '*¡Aviación!*' and leapt from the wagons. As I left the train I could hear a heavy drone overhead. I looked up, and there was a plane with its lights clearly visible, flying at the height of about three hundred feet. There was a flash, immediately followed by an explosion. A bomb dropped near the main road about half a mile from the village of Alcalá.

I made for a field and lay down as low as I could between plough-furrows. Some men must have still been running, as a voice near me shouted. 'Get down! *¡A tierra!*'

The plane circled and came back towards us, machine gun blazing away. I gripped the earth and held my breath. I could hear the bullets swishing near me, and I remembered being told: 'You don't hear the one that gets you.' I wondered if it were true. There was no anti-aircraft fire, and after a while the plane flew off over the sea to return no doubt to Mallorca. We returned to our wagons but had no sleep, as there were two false alarms within the next hour. The train then moved slowly away from the village and we were ordered to alight.

'Take your blankets and sleep in the open,' was the order. José and I, with two other Spaniards, chose a deep, dry ditch, and I enjoyed a few hours of the best sleep I had had since leaving Albacete. Shortly after midnight we were awakened and told to return to the train, which chugged along at a snail's pace until we reached Vinaroz.

As it grew lighter I could see the damage done to the station. There were large holes in the platform, and craters in the ground near the tracks. In a few places there were shiny new sections of track where repairs had been recently made. The sidings were filled with wrecked wagons and coaches.

'Let's see if we can find some clean water,' José suggested, and we left the station and walked towards some houses. The whole place was deserted, the inhabitants nowhere to be seen.

'They've been evacuated,' I said.

'Except the fascist fifth-columnists,' answered José. 'They'll be in hiding.'

At the rear of one empty house we found a rainwater tank where we had a good wash and shave and then returned to the train. We were told that as the train would not be leaving for some time we should go into the fields. I found a comfortable dry ditch and slept for a couple of hours in the warm sunshine. We had a meal of bread and corned beef and continued sleeping until the evening when we were recalled to the train and resumed our journey. As far as one could see, the whole countryside was deserted, except for troops. This meant that the advancing fascist army could not be far away and we wondered just how near they were.

There were bomb-craters in the fields near the railway track. Burnt-out wreckage of wagons, carriages and locomotives lay on both sides of the railway line. Alongside the road, which ran for miles parallel to the track, were smashed up lorries and cars. All the villages we went through were devoid of human life, though we saw stray dogs and cats in some.

At two o'clock in the morning on 10th April I was awakened by voices. Three or four men were standing by the wagon door.

'What's so interesting?' I asked.

'We're crossing the Ebro.'

I got up and joined the group. It was a clear night and the moon was shining brightly on the waters of the wide river. The train was going at no more than walking pace. To our dismay, the brakes were applied and it came to a halt on the bridge.

'Oh Christ! What the devil are they playing at?' asked one man.

'We must be a wonderful target for any fascist plane that's out tonight,' I said.

'Look,' yelled a Spaniard excitedly, 'you can see where the bridge has been damaged in previous raids.'

For a full ten minutes the train remained on the bridge. Then, at no more than three miles an hour, we crawled through

Tortosa station, which was badly damaged. I could see houses, whole sides of which had been torn off by bombs.

* * * * *

Once in Catalonia, the train gathered speed and we soon passed through Tarragona. From there to Barcelona we travelled through some of the most beautiful scenery I had ever seen. Emerging out of the many tunnels we would be presented with an unforgettable view – an inlet with the blue waters of the Mediterranean churning against black rocks or on a sandy bay. On each headland we could see sand-bagged trenches, part of Catalonia's coastal defences.

The first sight of Barcelona was also unforgettable. José García pointed out to me some of the landmarks, including the great avenues stretching from one side of the city to the other. Everywhere the population cheered and waved at us. We arrived at 2pm and were told that we could leave the train but must return to the station by nine o'clock.

José and Vicente Terol rushed to telephone relatives to tell them to come to the station. Vicente introduced me to his parents, a charming couple, but I soon left them as they naturally wished to be alone with him. As I walked away José called me. 'Here, comrade! Come and meet my brother-in-law.'

With his brother-in-law was a friend whose left arm was missing. He told us that he was on leave awaiting his discharge from the army. All four of us went into a café where José's brother-in-law produced a bottle of cognac, which we emptied. Then we drank vermouth and ate sardines and olives. We returned to Barcelona station and the train left at about 10pm. I awoke for a moment in the middle of the night to learn we were at Tarragona again. We were going back on the same line!

The morning of 11th April found us in Ampolla, a quaint fishing village by the side of the Mediterranean, some four or five railway stations south of Tarragona. We all went down to the pebbly beach where we sun-bathed and bathed in the sea. José García and I toured the old village, which reminded me rather of St Ives, a jumble of fishing-boats, women mending nets and old houses. We returned to the beach and slept for a while, after which we ate bread, sausage, chocolate, hazelnuts and biscuits.

In the afternoon there was an air-raid warning which disturbed García and me, as we were sleeping on a terrace at the side of the railway line. We went into a field about five hundred yards away, but, although we could hear anti-aircraft fire in the distance, the planes did not appear. On returning to the train, we were ordered to take our blankets once again into the fields.

José and I found a sheltering stone wall, made a fire on which we made a drink of Oxo (from a cube I had received from my mother), then went to sleep. The bugle-call to 'fall in' woke us again and my watch showed 2.30am. We returned to the coaches and to sleep, imagining that the journey was to be resumed.

When we awoke we were astonished to discover that we were still in Ampolla. I had come to the conclusion that we had been taken from Albacete in such a hurry that the Spanish government had not had time to make arrangements for us, that they did not know where to send us.

Then the train set off again and arrived in Tarragona, where we remained for about an hour and where we met some sailors from a British ship which had brought a cargo of wheat. One of them gave us a packet of Lucky Strike. From Tarragona we went south again, but this time we were switched to a branch line and turned inland.

Our journey finally ended at 11am on 13th April, after more than five days, in the town of Vilaseca where, on alighting, we were given a meal of bread, Spanish-style marmalade and nuts.

Corpse

There is no dignity in death;
nor is there beauty.
Staring eyes
do not command respect.
An open mouth
cannot give out commands.
A bloodless complexion
does not inspire affection.
Arms and legs
in an ungainly posture
would, in a circus ring,
be funny.
Here,
they are sad.

Battle Sounds

'Mine, mine, mine,'
whine
the rifle bullets,
leaden messengers of death,
claiming us as their prey
as we seek safety in the ditch
and hold our breath.
'Nay, nay, nay,'
say
the ricochets
that bounce from the grey rock
behind us, seeming to mock
our fears
as we press our nails into the protective clay.

Chapter 10 : Training again
13 April-20 May 1938

We formed fours and set off marching at a quick pace through Vilaseca. The people crowded in the streets and stared at us. Others gazed down from balconies. They must have seen plenty of soldiers before, but we were different.

'*Extranjeros*' (foreigners), I heard a man say to a woman.

'*Brigadas Internacionales,*' one of the Spanish soldiers shouted by way of explanation.

Immediately, the word went round and someone shouted: '*¡Vivan las Brigadas Internacionales! ¡Viva la República!*' The people on the pavement started cheering and clapping us.

'Let's give 'em a song,' suggested Joe Sloane, from London's East End, and started us off. Soon we were all singing as we marched:

> *Oh, we came to sunny Spain*
> *To make the people smile again,*
> *And to drive the fascist bastards*
> *From the hills and from the plain.*

It was a good, lively marching song, which we had all learnt back in Tarazona.

> *Mussolini sent some tanks.*
> *Franco thought that they were swell,*
> *Till we brought our anti-tank guns up*
> *And blew them all to hell.*

More people came out of the houses and shops to wave to us. Little children ran by our side, trying to keep pace. I was reminded of the reception we had had in Albacete and I thought that this one was more genuine because of its spontaneity. There were no flags and banners, but we really felt that the people of Vilaseca were glad to see us. We were marched through the town to a large field where we were halted and told to stand at ease. We all felt much better after the brisk march.

Alec Cummings called me over and pointed to a tree near one corner of the field. 'That's where we shall set up the 15th Brigade office. Now, who is going to help you and Vicente Terol? We're going to have a lot of clerical work very soon.'

I suggested José García, who, in turn, recommended Jaime Julia Suñén, who had come with him from Tarazona. Jaime was a well-educated Spaniard and very quietly spoken. Lieutenant Cummings agreed and the four of us started to take our boxes, typewriters, chairs and tables from an army lorry that had followed us from Vilaseca station. Meanwhile the rest of the men were sorted out into skeleton companies, ready for a draft of Spanish conscripts who, we were told, would arrive soon from Barcelona. One of the company commanders, I discovered, was Paddy O'Sullivan, whom I had known well in Tarazona. We were busy getting our open-air 'office' in order when there was a shout.

'*¡Aviación!*'

We all dashed to the edge of the field, where there was plenty of cover under the trees. As we lay on the ground we heard the drone of one plane. It came closer and dropped a bomb, which fell in a field about a hundred yards away. Then, in what seemed a matter of seconds, three Republican Air Force Polikarpov fighters appeared in the sky. The enemy turned and fled.

No more fascist planes appeared that day, and we were able to complete our arrangements. With canes from a nearby cane-break Jaime and José built a kind of hut round the trunk of the tree. This done, we moved in all the furniture and equipment and prepared lists of the men who had come with us.

Supper was late, so we turned in, and, when it did arrive, we ate it sitting on our blankets.

The following day we began the job of enrolling the Spanish recruits. Lorry-loads of young lads arrived throughout the day, and we had little rest.

Although my official position was camp interpreter, I spent a lot of time helping José and the other clerks to interview recruits. They were youngsters, eighteen-year-olds, and many of them were illiterate peasants, so we found that it was better if we filled in the enlistment forms for them and then asked them to sign them. Many did so with a thumb-print. We had been told to make lists of any who had special skills which might be useful, such as the ability to drive a car, handle mules and horses, or a knowledge of electricity. Many had worked with mules, but there were hardly any with other skills.

In the afternoon we were all marched to a nearby quarry for a political meeting. It was 14th April, the anniversary of the declaration of the Second Republic in 1931. The main speech, which I had to interpret, was delivered by the divisional commissar. He addressed himself to the young Spanish recruits, telling them that they ought to be proud to serve alongside the foreigners who had come of their own free will to defend the Republic. We were then given an issue of Raleigh cigarettes and told that we could have the rest of the day off.

After the meeting I walked into Vilaseca with a young Valencian. It is not a particularly beautiful town, but there were, at least, a couple of cafés where we drank vermouth. We then returned to the general store and purchased a kilo of hazelnuts. I bought a pair of rope-soled canvas shoes for nine pesetas. They would not have been more than five pesetas in Albacete.

The next day we were ordered to move our quarters to the quarry where the meeting had been held the day before. I was responsible for seeing the ammunition, rifles and the light machine guns moved safely.

Vicente and Jaime had gone on ahead to secure a good site for the HQ office and when I arrived I found a large hut built of canes and branches at the side of the quarry wall. No sooner had I entered than, once again, there was a shout of '*Vienen los aviones*' (Here come the planes) and we fell to the ground as the drone of planes came nearer. Three Italian *tri-motores* passed overhead in the direction of Vilaseca. Their bombs fell with thunderous explosions and were answered with anti-aircraft fire, which we could see was exploding short of the target. The three flew serenely away at a good altitude.

I climbed to the top of the quarry and saw a cloud of dust and smoke rising from Vilaseca. Evidently at least one bomb had made a hit. Later Joe Sloane, who had been in Vilaseca at the time, told me that the bombs had killed an old man, his granddaughter, a mule and a dog. Joe was a typical Cockney. He always seemed to know what was going on and had a knack of finding anything that was in short supply.[37]

When all the recruits had been enlisted and sent to the companies for basic military training, we could relax a little, and attend to personal hygiene. Jaime Julia found a stream some distance away and said that the water was clean, so one morning I went there to wash my clothes. I undressed completely, washed all the clothes and spread them on the hot ground. In less than half an hour they were dry enough to wear again.

* * * * *

On 16th April a message came from divisional HQ telling us that the following day (Sunday) would be a special fiesta in honour of the International Brigades and that we would be hosts to representatives of the Reus branch of the Association of Anti-Fascist Women. There would also be special food for breakfast and lunch.

On the Saturday night it rained a little, and we were glad of the partial protection offered by our cane hut. The day of the fiesta was dull and threatening. We had *mermelada* with our breakfast hunk of bread. This was not the gelatinous, bitter-sweet marmalade which I was used to eating in England, but thin, watery and sweet. It could not really be spread on the bread, so we dunked the bread in it, or drank it.

A few minutes before eleven in the morning the bugle sounded 'fall-in' and all the men assembled in front of a large flat slab of stone which served perfectly as a platform. The band of the Garibaldi Battalion played marches and revolutionary songs while we awaited our guests. When the Anti-Fascist Women of Reus arrived, there were expressions of admiration from many of the men, not for their undoubted anti-fascism, but because most of them were young and pretty.

The meeting opened with the playing of Spain's national anthem, after which the divisional commissar introduced the first speaker, the president of the Mujeres Antifascistas de Reus, and stated that she would present new colours to the division. She said she knew the 15th Brigade, who would receive the flag on behalf of the 35th Division, would defend it and all it represented, just as they had defended Madrid in the early days of the war.

The commissar of the division compared the ceremony with one held in Madrid in December 1936 when the Anti-Fascist Women of Madrid had presented a banner to the brigade. After the meeting, at which I interpreted, we were marched off to eat, and all wondered what the special meal would consist of. It turned out to be fried mule meat served with red peppers and, for dessert, a watery and not very sweet rice pudding.

In the afternoon the visitors returned and wandered round the camp, chatting with the solders. I was in great demand as an interpreter. Finally there was an open-air concert. Items included guitar and accordion solos and duets by 11th Brigade bandsmen, flamenco singing by the Spanish soldiers of the 15th Brigade and a recitation by a man of the 13th Brigade of García Lorca's *La casada infiel* (The Unfaithful Wife). This poem was a regular item at any impromptu concert. It was astonishing how many Spaniards knew it by heart. The poem was looked upon by most of the teenage Spanish soldiers not as great literature but as a dirty poem. They would grin lasciviously and wriggle nervously when the reciter reached the lines:

I touched her sleeping breasts
and like hyacinth buds
they opened at once to my caress . . .

By the middle of May the basic training of the recruits was completed and we were told that the Vilaseca camp was to be wound up. We were all going to join combat units.

* * * * *

On 20th May we left Vilaseca, travelling in open lorries through Reus and Barcelona to Terrassa, which we reached in the late afternoon. Shortly after our arrival, all the men were assembled and we were told that a senior officer of the 15th Brigade was going to make an important announcement. I was his interpreter. We both climbed onto a low stone wall, so that all the men could see and hear us.

'The Republic has gone through difficult times,' he told us. 'The fascists have, as you know, cut the country in two, and their advance towards Barcelona was only halted by the River Ebro, which gave our retreating forces time to reorganise.[38] At a time like this we must be constantly on the alert for spies, fifth-columnists, Trotskyists and defeatists. Only if they are completely eradicated will we be able to go forward to final victory.'

He paused after I had translated this. I could see the sea of upturned faces, and could read the expression in their eyes. This was not just the usual pep-talk. Clearly this high-up officer had something more to tell us. He looked at the assembled troops and spoke loudly and clearly, almost shouting to make sure he was heard.

'Today I have a very unpleasant duty to perform. I have to inform you that two of our comrades . . . No, I ought to say two men who pretended that they were our comrades have today been tried by court-martial and found guilty of deserting in the face of the enemy and of spreading defeatism. These two Trotskyists deserted during the fascist drive to the Mediterranean more than a month ago. They obtained civilian clothes and no doubt hoped to leave the country, but luckily they were picked up by the Servicio de Investigación Militar.[39]

'At first they denied that they were deserters from the International Brigades, but later admitted it.' He paused again, took off his glasses and polished them on a handkerchief. 'These two men have today been executed by firing-squad.'

After I had translated these words into English the parade was dismissed, but the men just stood there, still gazing in silence at the officer and me. Then a few started whispering and gradually the sound grew and grew until all were talking, arguing at the tops of their voices. The officer told me later that the two deserters were Scandinavians – he was not sure whether they were Finns or Swedes – and that the officer in charge of the firing-squad was none other than my friend Paddy O'Sullivan.

That evening there was only one topic of conversation. Most men agreed with the verdict and the sentence, but I wondered how many, in their hearts, felt as I did. Despite all that we had been told of defeatism, Trotskyism and fifth-columnists, I felt that these two men had really been executed merely because they were afraid and I wondered how afraid I would be when under fierce attack.[40]

The Songs We Sang

Oh, when I hear the sound of soldiers
singing, as they march along,
I hear again those stirring tunes
of 1930s marching songs.

Oh, when I hear the rhythmic beat
of soldiers marching down the street,
above the metronomic feet,
I hear those marching songs again,
the songs we sang in war-split Spain.

Our feet were noiseless as we marched;
our canvas shoes had soles of rope.
We seldom shaved; our hair was long
but in our hearts were songs of hope.

We did not swing our arms, as we
sang *Hold the Fort*, *No Pasarán*,
Come Workers Sing a Rebel Song and
Great Miaja Leads Us On.

Oh, when I hear a squad of soldiers
singing, then I think again
of all those friends who sang with me
the battle-songs of war-split Spain.

Chapter 11 : The Balaguer offensive
21 May-3 June 1938

On 21st May we moved again, but this time our journey was a short one. By midday the lorries had taken us to Cervera, where we were housed in an empty convent. It was a large stone building and a gloomy place, especially at night. All the furniture had been removed, but painted saints and angels looked down on us from the walls. We slept in a long first-floor gallery, the windows of which looked onto a quadrangle of grass and trees. The three days we spent at Cervera were sultry and oppressive, but we were cool at night, sleeping on the flagstones.

In the courtyard of the convent next day I asked one of the lorry-drivers when he thought we would join the rest of the 15th Brigade.

'I've not the foggiest idea, comrade,' he replied. 'Catalonia is so small that I could take you on a Cook's tour of the whole bloody place in a couple of days. I guess there's some reason why we haven't joined up with the combat units yet.'

'Maybe the brigade is in action,' I suggested.

'*¡Hombre!* Don't you follow the war bulletins? All is quiet on this front. It's more likely that the brigade, like us, is travelling round in lorries, awaiting orders to stop somewhere.'

While waiting we amused ourselves as best we could. From some of the British volunteers I had by now learnt a new slang expression – to organise. 'I'm going to organise some oranges' meant 'I'm going to pinch some oranges.' I do not ever remember anyone stealing anything valuable like money or tobacco in Spain. That would have been a serious crime and severely punished. But one 'organised' an extra ration from the kitchen, nuts or fruit from an orchard and it was considered no more serious than taking an apple from an orchard in Britain.

The three days in Cervera dragged, and we were bored, longing to reach our destination, before we were taken to Tárrega and I finally joined the British Battalion. I had travelled in the company of José García, Jaime Julia, Vicente Terol and some other Spaniards and, possibly for this reason or maybe because it was late at night and getting dark on 25th May, I was sent with them to join the Spanish rifle company of the British Battalion. The three 'British' companies contained about fifty per cent Spaniards; the Spanish company was one hundred per cent Spanish – until I joined it.

The company secretary made no comment when I spelled out my name to him, and I was sent to join a platoon under the command of a wiry little man from Aragón. He seemed delighted to have an Englishman in his platoon and he boasted about it to the other platoon leaders. For about a week we undertook quite vigorous training, going through the sort of military exercises that I had done in Tarazona.

Not only was my Spanish improving all the time, but I was also acquiring a good knowledge of vulgar Spanish. I soon discovered that none of the Spaniards I met ever said '¡Caramba!', '¡Dios mío!' or '¡Jesús!' Instead, the most commonly used words to denote surprise, disgust, pleasure, anger etc were '¡Joder!' and '¡Coño!' These were considered quite mild.

There was a lot of anti-religious feeling among Spaniards, who were disgusted with the Catholic Church for having sided with Franco against their legally elected government. This feeling was reflected in the oaths used, which generally began with the words '¡Me cago en . . . !' (I shit on . . .) The most common were '¡Me cago en Dios!', '¡Me cago en la Virgen'! and '¡Me cago en la hostia!', but Spaniards with more imagination would devise their own endings and occasionally one would hear a fluent Spaniard come out with a mouthful like, '¡Me cago en la madre del hijo de puta Franco!', or '¡Me cago en los veinticuatro cojones de los apóstoles!' When angry with someone else, a Spaniard might say '¡Me cago en la puta madre que te parió!' or '¡Me cago en la leche de tu madre!' These were very powerful insults and could often end in a punch-up.

* * * * *

On the last day in May the company commissar told us that the government was to launch an offensive near Balaguer and that, for the first time, the attack was not going to be spearheaded by the International Brigades. This was going to be an all-Spanish effort and the Republican Air Force was to give full support. He added that we were going to the front as reserve troops, to be used only if it proved necessary.

That afternoon we were taken to Mollerusa, where we made ourselves as comfortable as we could under the trees in a large field that lay between the main road and the railway line, about one mile east of the town.

As so often happened, when the news spread that there were International Brigades in the vicinity, the mayor of Mollerusa arranged a meeting in our honour. We, of course, were expected to go. We looked on these events rather as a British soldier might look on church parades, for we heard the same old speeches, no matter who the speaker was. The meeting in Mollerusa was held in a cinema and the main speaker was the mayor. He did not speak Spanish very well and, whenever he became excited, slipped into his native Catalan. At the end of his speech he worked himself up into a patriotic frenzy and concluded by shouting in Catalan: *'¡Visca la República Catalana!'* This caused the raising of several eyebrows. Although many Catalans hoped for complete separation from Spain, this was an aspiration not supposed to be voiced at that time, when the motto was 'Unity is strength'.

* * * * *

The next morning, Captain Sam Wild, commander of the British Battalion, came on a tour of inspection. He was accompanied by Bob Cooney, a red-faced Scot who was political commissar of the battalion. They conferred with my company commander and I could see that they were finding it hard to communicate. I strolled over to the group and said to Wild and Cooney: 'Do you need an interpreter, comrades?'

They admitted that they did, and I managed to get them over the language barrier. Then Sam Wild turned to me.

'Gracias, camarada. You speak very good English.'

'That's hardly surprising,' I replied, 'since I am English. I'm from Merseyside.'

'Then what the bloody hell are you doing in this unit?'

'This is where I was put when I joined the battalion at Tárrega.'

'Well, why didn't you tell us at the time that someone had made a mistake?'

'Comrade,' I answered. 'does it matter which company I'm in? We're all on the same side, aren't we?'

'You're right,' said Bob Cooney. 'But we can't leave you in the company, when other companies are badly in need of interpreters.'

'What were you trained as in Tarazona?' asked Wild.

'Machine gunner.'

'Good,' said Wild. 'It couldn't be better. Jack Nalty was complaining only yesterday that he had no interpreter. Okay, you'll be posted to another company, comrade.'

The next morning a runner came from battalion HQ with an order for me to report to Lieutenant Jack Nalty,[41] who was in command of the machine gun company. I walked up the slope to where Nalty and the company commissar, Tom Murray,[42] had their 'orderly room' under an almond tree. Jack was (I was later told by members of the company) a former member of the Irish Republican Army. He was pleased to have an interpreter and turned to his commissar.

'We'll make comrade Jump company secretary as well as interpreter. That will take some work from your shoulders, Tom.' Then, to me, he added: 'I'm glad to have someone who knows both languages. I can't talk English properly, let alone Spanish, and Tom's in the same boat. He's a Scot.'

Tom Murray was a patient, quiet-spoken man from Edinburgh. I got to know him well during the following three months. I never once heard him raise his voice, nor say a word in anger. He devoted much of his time to the welfare of the machine gunners. He told me that he was a lifelong teetotaller, so I was surprised to see him drinking red wine with his meals. I questioned him about this inconsistency.

'Back home I'd not drink anything alcoholic. But our diet at the present time is deficient. When autumn comes and there are plenty of grapes and oranges available, I'll not drink wine.'

He gave me an exercise book containing a list of all members of the company and another list of all arms – rifles, pistols and Maxims. There was also a bundle of forms on which I had to prepare a daily 'return' to battalion HQ.

Murray made me company postman, and this was a popular move. The mail came daily, often early in the morning, and the man who had previously had the job was fond of lying in his blanket until the very last moment. This meant that men sometimes had to wait longer than was necessary for letters and parcels from home. I was always an early riser, knew both Spanish and English and, what was more important, was able to decipher Spanish handwriting. I usually managed to distribute the mail before breakfast was over. I also had to assist at pay-parade and to help Tom Murray plan educational activities for the troops.

Soon after I joined the machine gun company the battalion was moved to higher ground nearer the Balaguer front line. There we could clearly hear the rumble of artillery fire and could feel the ground trembling during heavy bombardments. As we lay, hour after hour, expecting at any moment to be ordered into action, we could see, every half-hour or so, six Republican planes flying overhead in the direction of the front line. We would wait for the sound of exploding bombs, and then the planes would return. This, then, was the 'full support' of the air force.

For three days we awaited instructions to move to the front line, but the instructions never came. On 2nd June, the last day of our wait, we had a visit from Harry Pollitt, general secretary of the British Communist Party. All the English-speaking members of the battalion, rifles in hand or with Maxims close by, assembled on the terraces among the vines and Harry addressed us, starting something like this: 'I don't intend to talk politics. That would be presumption on my part, for it is you who are shaping politics and making history. I feel humble when I see you. So I'll give you a summary of the final positions in the Football League and the start of the cricket season.'

This was much more to our liking than hearing some politician telling us how brave we were and how proud he was of us. The cheer he received came straight from our hearts.

The noise of battle died down, and the rumour went round that the offensive had been a failure and had been called off. This seemed to be confirmed when, at dusk on the third day, we were put on lorries and driven for about seven hours in the dark. We had no idea where we were going.

At dawn the lorries pulled up and we were ordered to make ourselves as comfortable as possible in a *barranco*, a dried-up river-bed, of which there are many in Spain. We slept most of the morning and when we were told that we were likely to be there some time, the more energetic of us constructed shelters against the elements.

To a Comrade Sleeping

Sleep, sleep soundly, soldier,
for soon it will be morn
and we'll be back
in the attack
with tomorrow's summer dawn.

Drowse dreamlessly, comrade,
fast in your blanket cocoon
for, by daybreak, we must awake
and day will come all too soon.

Slumber sweetly, soldier;
no nightmare knit your brow.
Tomorrow's sleep
may be more deep
than the sleep you're sleeping now.

Sleep, sleep, soldier comrade!
May your sleep be sound!
Tomorrow night after the fight,
we may both sleep underground.

Chapter 12 : In the *barranco*
4 June-20 July 1938

For seven weeks, from 4th June to 20th July, the 15th Brigade remained in the dried-up river-bed near Marsá. From the start, it was clear that we were unlikely to be sent into action for some time. All was quiet on the Catalonian front. The daily war bulletins referred to air-raids by fascist planes and to artillery exchanges. The Republican army needed time to reorganise and the fascists, having reached the wide River Ebro, made no immediate attempt to cross.

We slept on the bare ground, wrapped in a poncho or greatcoat and one thin blanket. Many of the more energetic members of the British Battalion constructed shelters against possible rain – caves dug into the sides of the dry river banks or huts of branches and canes and roofed with clods of earth. I was one of the lazy ones. I used to sleep curled up under a tree. And I had the last laugh because the only rain we had was one very light shower that lasted no more than a quarter of an hour.

The afternoons were devoted to education or political activities, and all kinds of events were arranged by the political commissars. Sometimes these took the form of general discussions on political events. Whenever possible, the commissars tried to find an 'expert' to introduce the day's topic. On one occasion I was asked to give a talk on British newspapers; an ex-IRA man spoke on Irish nationalism; a Welsh miner, Billy Griffiths, gave a series of talks on dialectical materialism; and an American explained to us the organisation of US trade unions.

There were also classes of a purely educational nature – to teach Spanish to those British volunteers who were interested, or to teach Spaniards how to read and write. There were many illiterate men among the conscripts. For the most part they were country lads who had never had a chance to be educated. The ministry of education had published a special book to help them to learn to read and write. Instead of sentences about cars, dogs, children, mummy and daddy, they learned from such phrases as

'*La Unión Soviética nos ayuda*' (the Soviet Union helps us) and '*Saludamos la bandera de la República*' (we salute the flag of the Republic). Most of these students seemed to make rapid progress. One young Andalusian went straight from the *Cartilla escolar antifascista* (Elementary anti-fascist reader) to García Lorca's *Romancero gitano*, rather like graduating from 'The cat sat on the mat' to the poems of WH Auden.

Many Britons were not really enthusiastic about studying the Spanish language, being quite content to use the few words they had picked up. I used to teach a small group. Most afternoons they would sit in a circle on the ground, trying to master Spanish verb conjugations and syntax. It was difficult, as we had neither blackboard nor chalk and most men had no exercise books. Had we not possessed a few copies of the *15th Brigade Spanish Grammar* it would have been a quite hopeless task.

The political commissars were concerned not only with education, but also with the morale of the soldiers. Such matters as the quality of the food we were given and the prompt arrival and distribution of mail came under their aegis. They also had to be on the look-out for signs of racialism, anti-semitism, drunkenness and sexual deviation, all of which were considered to be serious offences. Excessive drinking, like catching venereal disease, was looked upon as a danger not only to the individual but to the Spanish People's Army. The atmosphere was, in fact, quite puritanical.

The official attitude to homosexual behaviour was even more severe. It was about this time, for example, that I missed seeing Vicente Terol, who had worked with me in the International Brigade's personnel office in Albacete. When I asked after him I could get no satisfactory answer. Much later I learned that Terol had been transferred to a labour battalion, after being found guilty of homosexual activity.

Drink was no problem with the Spaniards, who were used to drinking wine. Indeed, I never remember ever seeing a Spaniard who drank too much. Many Britons, however, tended to drink to excess. There was a tiny village about two miles from where we were encamped and some of the men wanted to go there for a drink ot an evening. Jack Nalty and Tom Murray insisted that no known heavy drinker should go unless accompanied by a teetotaller or a moderate drinker, who would be responsible for seeing that his charge did not get too drunk to find his way back to camp.

On a number of occasions I went with an Ayrshire comrade, John Smith. I used to wonder how he could possibly drink so much without being sick. He would get slightly tipsy, but never gave me any real trouble, though he would become sentimental and homesick and, in a discordant, cracked voice, would sing *My Ain Folk* with tears in his eyes. When I thought he had had enough I would persuade him to return and we would walk down the lane in the blackness of the night singing *I Belong to Glasgow*.

I never came across much racialism nor anti-Jewish feeling, though on one occasion I attended the 'trial' of an Irishman who was accused of anti-semitism because, in the heat of an argument, he had called a comrade a 'stinking fucking Jew'. He was brought before Jack Nalty and Tom Murray, who listened carefully to the complainant. The accused man admitted using the words and expressed regret. He was 'sentenced' to make a public apology to his comrade, after which they shook hands and went off together sharing a cigarette, which non-smoker Tom gave them.

As we were awakened every morning at half-past five, we had plenty of time for military training before the midday heat made running about almost impossible. We had firing practices, perfected our handling of the machine guns and learned the art of camouflage. Besides the Maxims, and the rifles which were carried by all men who did not belong to a gun crew, our company was issued with two brand-new mortars, which all of us were keen to fire.

This new mortar was a very simple weapon consisting of a steel tube about two and a half feet long, with a firing-pin at the bottom. When it had been 'aimed' by getting the correct angle on a gauge marked in tens of metres from three to twenty-five, the mortar-bomb was placed in the top of the barrel and allowed to drop down the tube. On the pin striking the detonator, the bomb was fired. We were warned to take our hands away from the barrel the moment we dropped the bomb, or we would have a hand blown off. We used to climb with the mortars up the steep hills on one side of the valley and lob mortar-bombs over the *barranco* at targets on the opposite range of hills.

* * * * *

We always sang when we marched to and from manoeuvres or military training sessions. Our songs included American labour songs like *Hold the Fort*. We also had our own words to suit the occasion. To the tune of *She Wore a Yellow Ribbon* we would sing:

> *Franco thought that he could take the nation;*
> *Then up stood Miaja with his Red Army.*
> *When we look into the situation*
> *We can see that not far away is our victory.*

There was also a Spanish version of the French song *La Jeune Garde* and the medical unit of the 15th Brigade sang Spanish words to the French song *La Madelon*. There were many specially written Spanish songs such as *Miliciano popular* and *Juventudes proletarias*, while others were old folk-songs to which new words had been put. Such was the *Canción de la Quince Brigada*:

> *Viva la Quince Brigada, rumbala, rumbala, rumbala;*
> *Está cubierta de gloria ¡Ay, Manuela! ¡Ay Manuela!*

We also sang round camp-fires in the evening. A group of ten or twelve sitting cross-legged in a circle would, in turn, sing a song for the rest to join in. All the evergreen music-hall songs like *Daisy Bell (Bicycle Built for Two)* and Harry Lauder ballads, Irish songs (James Connolly's *A Rebel Song* was a favourite), Welsh hymns and Spanish folk-songs were included in our repertoire.

Jesús Poveda taught me the words of many songs, such as *La golondrina*, *Me dejaron de herencia mis padres* and *Eres alta y delgada.* Jesús was a poet from Orihuela, where he had been employed in local government before joining the army. At the end of the war he was interned in Saint-Cyprien.[43] I received this news from another poet, Eduardo de Ontañón, who was brought to England with a group of intellectuals and who later went to Mexico. I wrote to Jesús's home in Orihuela after the end of the war, but received no reply. He probably lost his life in the Second World War when France was occupied by the Nazis.

Rafael Garmendia Gil, one of the young Spanish conscripts, was a born comedian and everyone liked him. He had a crew-cut – very hygienic in those conditions – and this had the effect of accentuating his large ears. He was a clever mimic and, though he had no knowledge of English, he used to entertain us with an impersonation of an eminent English-speaking politician addressing the battalion. These politicians all said much the same thing and Rafael, from repeatedly hearing the same phrases, was able to imitate them. His speech, accompanied by comical gestures, used to have us in fits of laughter. It went something like this: 'Comrades, blah-blah-blah, freedom fighters, blah-blah, Spanish legal government, blah-blah-blah, fascist criminals, blah-blah, traitor Franco, blah-blah, Italian soldiers, blah-blah, German planes, blah-blah, bloody murderers, blah-blah, victory will come, blah-blah, freedom, blah-blah, *no pasarán.*'

In fact we were generally bored to tears by these eminent visitors, who included Ellen Wilkinson (later to become Minister of Education in Attlee's postwar administration), Álvarez del Vayo (Foreign Minister of the Spanish Republic), Hewlett Johnson (the 'Red' Dean of Canterbury) and Earl Browder (Secretary of the US Communist Party).

Exceptions were those visitors who stepped down from the platform and mingled with the troops. One of these was Pandit Nehru, who later became president of India and who came accompanied by Krishna Menon (later India's Foreign Minister) and Joseph P Kennedy, elder brother of John F Kennedy. Nehru spent quite a long time in the *barranco*, chatting to us. He displayed great interest, despite being a pacifist, in our machine guns, and the gun crew, led by ex-miner from Fife, George

Jackson, put on an exhibition of accurate firing. With a few short bursts of fire from their First World War Maxim, they chopped down a sapling growing a couple of hundred yards away.[44]

'Would you like to have a try yourself?' Jackson asked him, but Nehru politely refused.

Years later I was told by Bob Doyle that eminent British visitors also went to Franco's Spain. When Doyle was a prisoner of war at San Pedro de Cardeña, near Burgos, the prisoners had a visit from Lady Chamberlain, sister-in-law of the British prime minister, Neville Chamberlain. Accompanied by a high-ranking Spanish officer she inspected the prisoners who were lined up on parade and she asked each one where he was from and why he had gone to Spain. Apparently dissatisfied with the answers she received, she turned to the officer and said: 'Do you think you could pick me an intelligent one?'[45]

Another visitor at the *barranco* was Edward Heath, who eventually became a Conservative prime minister. He arrived with a delegation from the National Union of Students. With him was a student named George Bean who, after the speech-making and the singing of *El Himno de Riego* and *The Internationale*, spoke to Sam Wild. 'I'd very much like to have my photo taken with any Merseyside men in the battalion.'

Those of us who came from Liverpool, Birkenhead, Bootle and Wallasey gathered round the visitor and the picture was later published in the *Liverpool Echo*.[46] Little did any of us guess at the time that the slim, young Liverpool docker and Labour councillor in the group, James Larkin 'Jack' Jones, would later lead the Transport and General Workers' Union.

I met Joe Moran again in the *barranco*. I had not seen him since Tarazona. The young man who, when he went to Spain, had no idea whom or what he was going to fight against, had changed completely, and had even joined the Spanish Communist Party. He had a mania for sunbathing and, naturally dark-skinned, was as swarthy as a Spanish gypsy. Most days our breakfast consisted of 'coffee' and bread fried in olive oil. After breakfast, Joe used to go to the metal containers which had been used to bring the food from the cookhouse, rub his hands on the oil inside, and anoint his body – chest, shoulders, arms and legs. It was he, too, who started the fashion of converting his long trousers into shorts. Rafael Garmendia was quick to follow Joe's fashion.

One Sunday afternoon Rafael came and told me that he wanted to introduce me to his parents and sister. I went with him and there, on the road above the *barranco*, I saw a smartly dressed couple and a pretty girl of about fourteen or fifteen. We chatted for a while, but Rafael's sister Elena would only speak to him. She was very shy and I could get nothing but monosyllables from her. The father produced a wine-skin and we all drank the tar-flavoured red wine. This was the first time I had ever used one and at my first attempt I squirted the wine all over my face, whereupon Elena was told off by her father for laughing at me.

When they returned to Barcelona I asked Rafael how his parents had discovered where the brigade was stationed. All our mail was censored and it would have been impossible to send a letter containing the sentence: 'We are in a *barranco* near Marsá.' With a twinkle in his eyes, he explained.

'Look,' he said, taking a used envelope from his pocket. 'In Spain we must write on the back of an envelope the name and address of the sender.'

'I know that,' I said.

'Well, my full name is Rafael Garmendia Gil, Gil being my mother's surname, but when I wrote home a couple of weeks ago I put on the back 'Rafael Garmendia Marsá. My parents twigged it and came to see me.

Early in July, the training sessions became more and more strenuous and we gained an inkling of what was in store for us. Manoeuvres always included an imaginary river-crossing. When, in mid-July, all sailors were transferred from the battalion it was quite obvious that there was to be an offensive across the Ebro. But when?

Ebro Offensive, 24th July 1938

Soon we shall launch the attack.
This is no routine manoeuvre.
We must regain
the ground we lost three months back.

All my belongings have gone in a lorry
to the safety of the rear
and I am alone,
wearing my tattered uniform and my fear.
In my pockets I have nothing of my own –
not even a pocket-knife or comb.
I have no money and not a single photograph
to transport me, temporarily
from the war.
I have a 1908 rifle,
fifty cartridges stuffed in my pockets
and two hand-grenades tied to my belt.
In my blanket-roll I have a loaf of bread
and a tin of corned beef.
My tin mug and water-bottle are securely tied
so that they will not rattle when I run,
crouching,
in my rope-soled sandals
or crawl on my belly
like an ungainly tailless lizard.

If I am lucky and come out of the front line
in, maybe, ten days' time,
I shall have my own things again –
a book of Lorca poems,
a badge in the colours of Republican Spain,
Cayetana's photograph,
a fountain-pen and a change of socks.
But first, we have to launch the attack.

Cayetana Lozano Díaz.

Chapter 13 : Across the Ebro
20-26 July 1938

Tom Murray woke me on 20th July by grabbing my shoulder and shaking me. The night was pitch black. 'We're leaving here. Give me a hand to go round and tell the comrades. They must be packed up and ready to leave in half an hour.'

In less than that time the whole company was ready. We marched up to the road, which ran parallel to the *barranco* near Marsá. Many of the men were complaining.

'Hell, another bloody manoeuvre!'

'It might be the real thing this time.'

'Stuff it! Don't start any shit-house rumours.'

'Tom Murray says it might be the real thing.'

'Bollocks! He doesn't know anymore than we know.'

'Well, he says we're going to the front line.'

All doubts were quickly dispelled when we were issued with live ammunition and two hand-grenades each. Those of us who carried rifles were each given twenty-five cartridges. Having no ammunition pouches, we stuffed them into our pockets; the grenades we tied to our belts.

We boarded the waiting lorries and were driven off into the night. It was a slow journey, as the vehicles' lights could not be lit. We travelled through Falset, where the HQ of the 15th Brigade was, and at last arrived, just before dawn, at Gratallops. We were told to take cover in a *barranco* near the village. We were warned not to move around in the open in case any enemy reconnaissance planes were about. We saw plenty of these planes and remained under cover of bushes and trees.

During the night we were marched some ten or twelve miles to yet another dried-up river-bed not far from La Torre del Español, where we remained for three days. I wrote a number of letters to my parents, my fiancée Cayetana, my brother Jack and to friends in Sussex. It might be the last chance I would have for some time. We were very busy making preparations, each man checking that his arms were in perfect working order. I recalled our marching song in Tarazona that ended:

For on our rifles depends our freedom.
¡No pasarán! ¡No pasarán!

We packed all our personal belongings into our haversacks and these were taken away on a lorry for safe-keeping. Not that we had many personal effects; mine comprised a photograph of my fiancée, a few letters from her and from my parents, a few pesetas, one or two books and a spare pair of socks. My lighter and tobacco went into the breast-pocket of my shirt, where I already had four or five rounds of ammunition.

On the last day some mules arrived, one for each machine gun crew and, under the direction of the muleteers, the gunners learned how to pack the heavy guns and the boxes of ammunition on the backs of the animals.

It was on 24th July when, at eleven at night, we were marched from the river-bed. The narrow lanes, empty of traffic during the day, were now choked with marching troops and vehicles of all kinds. On some of the lorries we spotted rowing-boats and pontoons. Before dawn we reached a cane-break, where I managed to snatch a couple of hours of sleep.

At dawn we were awakened by the noise of gunfire coming from the direction of the River Ebro, which Jack Nalty told us was about a quarter of a mile away. We were given breakfast, after which each man was issued with a loaf of bread and a tin of corned beef. We had no idea how long this would have to last us. A lorry with a large water tank drove up, and we filled our water-canteens.

I wondered whether the offensive would be successful, or would it peter out like the Balaguer offensive had done. Tom Murray explained to us that the government had decided to launch an attack across the Ebro on a wide front, from Mequinenza down to the sea, to relieve pressure on the Valencian front. Franco's progress along the coast towards the city had, in fact, been very slow, thanks to the dogged resistance put up by the Republican troops.

'Everything depends on the success of our offensive,' he said.

'The preparations have been thorough. I have been informed that our intelligence has obtained complete details of the defences of the fascist forces defending the Ebro – even down to the names of the commanding officers of the military formations. If the enemy has been taken by surprise it should be possible for us to advance deep into enemy territory in a very short time. If there is no surprise element in our attack, then it will be a very bloody affair.'

James R Jump (standing, second from right) with other members of the British Battalion at Marsá in July 1938, along with George Bean (standing in foreground, with jacket) and Jack Jones (third from left, in leather jacket).

Each company was issued with two flags, the red, yellow and purple flag of the Republic, and the red and yellow flag of Catalonia. Our instructions were to display the one which was the most appropriate in any given circumstances. Tom Murray explained what this meant. 'To identify ourselves to Republican forces we shall display the Republican flag. The Catalan flag, four red stripes on a yellow background, could easily be mistaken for the fascist flag, two red stripes on a yellow background.'

We listened intently, half-guessing what he would say next. 'If fascist planes or troops mistake the Catalan flag for their own, it's not our fault. We're not flying false colours.' This ruse appealed to us all, but we wondered whether it would prove effective. It sounded crazy.

Jack Nalty and Tom Murray decided that I ought to carry the flags. As they were very large – about four and a half feet by three feet, I decided that I would, therefore, leave my blanket with my haversack and use the two flags as blankets. By half-past seven the noise of gunfire had died down and we were told that the initial attack had been successful. This cheered us up.

Jack Nalty called a meeting of officers and NCOs to brief them. I attended as interpreter. 'The enemy is in full retreat along the whole of this front. We shall be crossing the river as soon as orders are received.'

'How do we cross the Ebro?'

'In rowing-boats. Work has already begun on a pontoon bridge, but it is a long way from completion.'

'Thank Christ they don't expect us to swim across!' someone muttered.

'When we get to the other side we shall march towards Gandesa, avoiding contact with the enemy. Our first aim is to occupy as much fascist territory as possible.'

'Don't we have to wipe the bastards out, Jack?'

'Not unless they stand in the way of our advance. Any pockets of resistance will be cleaned up by the troops that follow us.'

A runner arrived, breathless, from battalion HQ and handed Jack Nalty a note, which he read.

'This is it boys. Good luck to all of you.'

The meeting broke up, and the officers and NCOs returned to take charge of their gun crews and mules.

In a long line we walked along a narrow path through the twelve-feet-tall canes until we reached a pebbly beach. In front of us was a broad stretch of slow-moving water. Beyond that, on the far side of the river, we could see the low-lying land which, only an hour or so previously, had been in enemy hands.

Jack Nalty, Tom Murray, two runners, two first aid orderlies and I crossed in the first boat. Behind us came boats carrying the gun crews. Each of these boats was towing a mule, whose head only could be seen as it swam behind. There was an Italian plane circling overhead, but no bombs were dropped while we were crossing. A little way upstream we could see men working on the construction of a pontoon bridge. It was still far from complete, reaching only about a quarter of the way across the river.

On reaching the opposite bank, we leapt from the boat into about a foot of water and climbed up the shingle. Near the water's edge I saw two enamel plates, upturned side by side on the ground. 'Don't touch them!' warned Jack. 'It may be a booby-trap.'

We waited under cover of some low bushes until the whole company had crossed and the machine guns had been placed on the backs of the mules. Then we started to march, across fields at first and then along the road leading to Corbera. Everywhere we could see signs of the enemy having left in a great hurry. By the sides of the road were blankets, bits of uniforms, haversacks, and even a gramophone. On our flanks we could hear the sound of gunfire from time to time.

Occasionally we passed farms, and saw small groups of people, mostly women, children and old men.

'¡Salud! ¡Viva la República!' we shouted in greeting.

'¡Viva la República!' they replied, raising their clenched fists.

One woman detached herself from a group and ran over to us, offering us big ripe plums from a basket. We took them gratefully and thrust into her basket all the change we had in our pocket.

We marched at a rapid pace and were soon sweating. I wondered how far we would be able to advance like this before we came up against stiff resistance. Only then were we to dig in and form a line by making contact with the troops on each side of us. All morning and most of the afternoon we marched in two files, one on each side of the road. I was displaying the red and yellow flag of Catalonia, and it seemed that the ruse was successful. Every now and then an enemy plane circled overhead, but we were not attacked.

'They don't know whether we're Republicans, or fascists retreating,' commented Tom Murray. Soon, however, we had a rude awakening. An enemy plane circled overhead for a few minutes, and then suddenly dropped out of the sky like a guillemot diving for fish and came towards us, machine guns blazing away.

'Get down!' yelled Jack Nalty.

'*¡A tierra!*' I heard Spanish voices shout.

I lay down in the shallow ditch at the side of the road and pressed my body as hard as I could against the hot, dry earth. Then the plane departed and I could relax a bit. I looked around. Either the gunner's aim was bad or we were lucky, for no-one had been hit.

'I think I'd better hide these flags,' I said, and those near me agreed, so I rolled them up and stuffed them into my shirt. From the rear came the sound of bombs exploding in the distance, and we guessed that the fascists were trying to destroy the pontoon bridge. We wondered whether it had been completed. We would be in a very unpleasant situation if no vehicles could get across the river. In the late afternoon, however, we were overtaken by an ambulance and a Republican army lorry. This made us all feel happier.

We halted, and were glad to sit down and rest on the grass by the roadside. This rest also gave us a chance to open our tins of meat and eat something. While we were resting, a message was received by Jack Nalty. It stated that the 13th Brigade had reported that they were unable to enter Corbera because the road was under fire from some fascist troops on a hill to our left. The British Battalion had been given the task of clearing them out.

We moved cautiously towards the hill, taking cover behind hedges and bushes. Company HQ was set up in the shelter of a low stone wall and Jack told me to stay near him in case he needed an interpreter. We watched the men move slowly forward until they were near the summit of the hill. We waited, bullets screeching over our heads. The rifle fire became more intense and we could hear short bursts of machine gun fire, followed by explosions of hand-grenades. The whole operation lasted until dark. Then there was a sudden eerie silence as the firing ceased.

We had suffered a few casualties. One of those killed was Gordon Bennett of Birmingham, who had enlisted in the International Brigades with his elder brother Donald. When Donald returned from the hill after the battle I saw him weeping openly. He had apparently been with Gordon and seen him shot.[47]

Some of the men brought back with them the identity documents of the dead fascist soldiers, and from these we learned that they were Moorish troops serving in the Spanish Legion. We spent the night at the foot of the hill. I slept in the two flags.

* * * * *

At sunrise we continued our advance and soon reached Corbera, which was now safely in Republican hands, but we did not enter the town. Instead we veered to the left and after crossing some fields, rejoined the Gandesa road on the other side of Corbera.

We plodded on, thirsty and hungry, for we had no food left, having finished the bread and corned beef the night before. As we neared Gandesa, Caproni bombers flew overhead. On a number of occasions we had to scatter and hide in ditches. Sometimes I could hear the whistle of the bombs as they fell, always wondering if one of them 'had my name on it'. We seemed to be lucky, as we suffered no casualties in these attacks, either because the bombing was inaccurate or because we were not the target. The planes certainly had plenty of other things to aim at – ambulances, lorries, motorcyclists and staff cars. The roads, in fact, were crowded. Cavalry troops had no need to stay on the roads. They went across the open country. They made a fine sight, but I doubt if their military value was very great.

We again turned off the Gandesa road and walked in single file up a zig-zag track flanked by rough stone walls. I noticed that everyone was stooping and walking about like Groucho Marx. This surprised me as I could hear no gunfire, but I decided that I'd better do the same. I wondered what we were sheltering from and, indeed, in which direction the enemy lines lay. I had quite lost my bearings.

'What are we sheltering from?' I whispered to one of the medical orderlies. (I have no idea why I whispered; at the time it seemed the sensible thing to do.)

'Christ knows,' came the reply.

As we reached the higher ground, those ahead began to walk upright and I followed suit. It was a relief to straighten my back. We had to scatter and find shelter as two planes flew over and dropped four bombs very near us. It was in this attack that one of our mules was wounded, and had to be killed. Now it was the turn of the gun crew to carry the Maxim and ammunition. George Jackson shared the parts among the members of his crew, and kept the heaviest for himself. He was a tall, strong man and seemed to carry with ease what I could scarcely lift.

We had another brief halt, and Jack Nalty put us into the picture.

'The quick advance is over,' he said. 'Gandesa is not going to fall without a fight. However, I've had some good news. Our field kitchen has crossed the Ebro and is not far behind us, so maybe we'll get a square meal soon.'

'Meal? What's a square meal?' said someone. 'My guts have forgotten what food is.'

'Now get ready for some mountaineering,' Jack said, pointing to some mountains ahead. 'We're going to the top of those. That's where the front line is.'

Sun over the Front

The sun adds to our plight
as we lie, face down, on the angry earth.
We sweat and,
like misers, conserve our dwindling supply of water,
by now sickly warm.
We shall receive no more before night.
Deliriously I dream of floating away. I dream
of cool sea breezes. I dream
of stretching in deep grass beneath sycamore shade. I dream
of lying naked in a fast-flowing mountain stream.
In the sun's face of incandescent brass
there is no smile of compassion.
His hot breath rustles the dry grass
and brings to our lines
the scent of pine,
broom and mountain thyme.
The sun smiles no pity on the wounded
out in no-man's land.
An invisible curtain of potential bullets
hangs between them and us.
Enemy machine guns warn off
our stretcher-bearers but do not ward off
the sun's vibrant stare.
Our comrades' groans
and pleas for help are brought to us on the warm air.
'Madre mía! Madre mía!' one cries. 'Water!' another moans.

At last the sun dries
the moisture on their tongues
and evaporates their cries.
By my side
a young Spanish conscript crosses himself,
his lips moving rapidly
without a sound

Now the suffocating silence is frightening.
We try to forget our friends out there;
we make ourselves think of our own plight
as we lie, face down, on the angry earth.
We force ourselves to think of our own fight
against the sun.

Chapter 14 : The battle for the Pimple
27 July-6 August 1938

It must have taken us a couple of hours, scrambling up narrow rocky tracks, to reach our positions high in the Sierra de Caballs. The mules made light work of it, but George Jackson's gun crew sweated as they climbed, carrying the heavy Maxim. Those of us who had little to carry – Tom Murray, Jack Nalty, the runners and me – took turns to help them. There were some parts of the gun that I could scarcely lift, such as the carriage with its cast-iron wheels, but we helped with the ammunition and the shield.

At last we reached the summit and far below we could see the town of Corbera, a cluster of red roofs round a church tower. We advanced along a ridge and came at last to the 'front line'. There was, in fact, no continuous line. We were ordered to 'dig in', and I recalled Major Allan Johnson's talks in Tarazona about the consolidation of conquered terrain. It was quite impossible to dig in; all we could do was build parapets and firing positions out of large jagged rocks. There was no soft earth for our sandbags, so we filled them with small stones.

Before us lay the town of Gandesa, surrounded on three sides by troops of the International Brigades and part of a Spanish division commanded by General Enrique Líster. At first glance it looked as though Gandesa could easily be captured. Between us and the town, however, was Hill 481, which we nicknamed the Pimple. Hill 481 was heavily fortified. The fascists had observation posts and artillery positions which dominated the slightly lower ground which we held. They rained shells on our positions, while squadrons of Italian and German bombers were continually overhead. Later I read that they were dropping ten thousand bombs a day on the Republican lines. We certainly had our share of these.

Time after time the 15th Brigade (British, Americans and Canadians) supported by the 13th Brigade, largely composed of Slavs, and the Spaniards under Líster tried to dislodge the fascists from this key hill, but every time we were driven back.

British losses were heavy. Jack Nalty was wounded and the command of his company was taken over by the adjutant, another Irishman, Paddy Duff. Then he too was wounded.

I was some thirty yards to the rear with Tom Murray when I saw Paddy staggering down the slope. Both his arms were covered with blood, which was running down his arms and dripping from his fingers to the ground.

'Are you all right, Paddy,' I said, running forward to assist him.

'I can manage,' he answered, but he was swaying, and I could see that he was on the point of falling.

'Come on. Let me help you,' I said. I supported him and, together, we slowly make our way towards battalion HQ, where on a mound I saw Sam Wild, binoculars in hand, watching the progress of the battle. I handed Paddy over to a medical orderly and then returned to the front line. My uniform was covered in blood.

I was, of course, afraid when I went into action for the first time, but everyone had told me that this was only to be expected. Lying in a ditch, or seeking cover between the furrows of an open field while Italian and German bombs were falling or when enemy fighter-planes dived on our positions, machine guns blazing, one's first instinct is to get up and run. This is to invite death. It is safer to lie still.

I cannot remember being afraid of death itself, though I realised that this was more than just a possibility. What scared me more was the thought of being badly wounded. The idea of being blinded or losing a limb quite terrified me at times.

Later, I had an even greater fear – that of being injured and lying in an exposed position where rescuers could not reach me. During the first attacks on Hill 481 we had all heard the moans and cries of '¡Agua!' (water) '¡Socorro!' (help) and '¡Ay, madre mía!' coming from the wounded in no-man's land – cries that became weaker and weaker as the poor fellows – were they fascist or Republican? – sank into unconsciousness.

* * * * *

It was during the battle for the Pimple that I came to the conclusion that I would never make a real soldier. I had often remembered the expressions on the faces of the British volunteers when I translated for them the news of the execution of the two Scandinavians some months before. Those two men had been labelled Trotskyists – a label so easily fastened on anyone who deviated from the 'correct' political line. Most of my comrades seemed to agree, but I suspected that the condemned men were victims of their own fear. They had been terrified out of their lives and, unable to stand anymore, had deserted. I had been terrified too, and I knew what it felt like.

Then one evening, after yet another fruitless attempt to take the Pimple, I learned how Paddy O'Sullivan had shot a young Spaniard, a would-be deserter. According to the story, Paddy, during a lull in the fighting, had come across an eighteen-year-old conscript hiding in some bushes. He had ripped all identification markings from his uniform and had thrown away his rifle. It was clear to Paddy that the lad intended to wait until darkness fell and then try to reach the fascist lines. Maybe his parents were living in enemy-occupied territory.

Paddy ordered him to return to our positions. The Spaniard either refused or displayed unwillingness to obey the command, whereupon Paddy drew his revolver and shot him through the head. I listened to the comments of my comrades.

'It serves the little bastard right.'

'It's the only way to deal with bloody Trotskyists.'

That was the moment when it dawned on me that I would never be a real soldier like Paddy O'Sullivan. I felt sure that I could never have shot a Spaniard in cold blood as Paddy had done. Yet, at the same time, I had no idea what I would have done in his place. Would I have tried to reason with him? Would I have turned a blind eye? These questions I could not answer to my satisfaction.

I came to the conclusion that I was only intellectually an anti-fascist. I knew that fascism was evil. All that I had read convinced me that under a Nazi or fascist regime the individual would count for nothing. But this anti-fascist feeling came from the head, not the guts. Politically speaking, I sometimes felt almost ashamed of myself and my thoughts.

All around me were men who had suffered poverty and unemployment, and the degradation that accompanied those two evils. These men were capable of hatred and revenge. To them, fascism was an extension of capitalism, under which they had suffered hardship and humiliation. They were coal-miners from Scotland and South Wales, hunger-marchers from the shipyards of the North-East, Irish Republicans who felt that their cause had been betrayed by De Valera. They had not become socialists through reading *Left Review* or the *New Statesman*.

Maurice 'Paddy' Ryan, a big, round-faced man of about my own age whom I had got to know shortly before we crossed the Ebro, had an irrepressible sense of humour and he revered no one. In the lulls in the fighting Paddy and I used to talk a lot, and some comrades were a little shocked by what Paddy used to say. He was always joking, and often directed his jokes against the International Brigade administration and the Communist Party. His jokes were harmless enough but they disconcerted the more loyal party members.

To the Great War defeatist song *I Want To Go Home*, which in the Second World War became famous as *Bless 'Em All*, Paddy put his own ribald words poking gentle fun at the Young Communist League. I heard some YCL'ers call him, among other things, a defeatist, a traitor and even a Trotskyist – the worst possible insult.

Paddy had a brother who had been recruited by General O'Duffy and was serving in Spain in the general's Blueshirts, the Irish Brigade.[48] Paddy shocked us all one day when he said: 'All I hope is that in battle one of these days I meet that fucking bastard face to face.'

On another occasion he said in a loud voice: 'Why can't they teach me a decent trade like motor maintenance? All I've learnt in this bloody army is how to fire a machine gun. What the hell's the use of that when I get home. I'll not be qualified to do anything except join the fucking IRA.'

This did not go down well with the many members of the IRA in the ranks of the British Battalion. When I was told that Paddy had been executed by firing-squad for Trotskyism the news quite sickened me, for I liked him and did not believe that there was any real bad in him. He was a brave soldier and a fine machine gunner when he was not sleeping off the effects of drinking too much wine. His only fault, and in wartime it is a fault, was that he would not 'toe a political line'. Paddy said what he thought and, if the powers that be did not like it, it was just too bad. He was incapable of keeping silent when prudence demanded it. I could not help wondering who had formed the firing-squad. Was it possible that Paddy's own comrades shot him, or had Spaniards been selected?[49]

* * * * *

Our biggest attack on the Pimple came on 1st August, and I shall never forget the horror of it. It was pandemonium. Shells and bombs rained on our lines all morning and most of the afternoon. Shrapnel shells burst overhead and bullets whistled past us, sometimes whining like fireworks when they ricocheted off the rocks. It seemed impossible that anyone could live through such a storm of metal. Many men were killed, as were also our remaining mules.

Lewis Clive, Kensington Labour councillor and author of *The People's Army*, died in this battle.[50] Another to be killed was David Guest, a mathematician.[51] He was the son of the MP Leslie Haden-Guest. David was just about the most unmilitary person one could imagine. In the British Army he would have been the despair of any corporal, but he was a great comrade, and brave.

Paddy O'Sullivan was badly wounded, and died before he could be brought back from no-man's land, where he lay for more than an hour, moaning under the hot sun. That night the bodies of the dead were laid in shallow graves. There was no wind and the sickly-sweet smell of blood and putrefaction hung over the front line. Someone remarked: 'Do you know what day it is in England?'

No-one answered. We were too tired.

'Bank holiday,' he said.

I felt a little homesick, and I think most of the other men shared my feelings,

The battles for the Pimple continued for five more days and more of my friends were killed. They included John Smith, who had been a good companion on evenings off in the *barranco* at Marsá and a brave soldier, though he confessed to me that he had volunteered to fight in Spain for three things – drink, women and loot – and had not found much of either.[52] Among those wounded badly enough to be sent to hospital was Bill Harrington, who had been the assistant paymaster at Tarazona.

We were worn out, thirsty, hungry and filthy. There was never enough water to drink, let alone wash and shave with. To quench our thirst we tried chewing tiny green grapes from some vines growing on the lower slopes, now left untended because of the battle, but they were sour and gave us stomach-ache.

The cookhouse boys did their best but meals arrived at irregular times and often they were strange, unsatisfying meals. A lot of tinned food had been captured in a fascist army store at Corbera and for days we were eating tins of Portuguese sardines, watery Spanish jam and corned beef, but too often there was no bread to go with these luxuries.

There were rumours that, although the offensive had been successful along the whole of the bend of the Ebro, further north things had not gone well. At Mequinenza the fascists had surrounded and captured a large Republican force. This was confirmed when we had a leaflet-raid. The leaflets that were dropped from enemy planes threatened in Spanish that the same fate awaited us, and urged us to desert to the fascists.

Most of the British could not, of course, understand what was printed on the leaflets, but, as some of them were printed on very thin paper, they gathered them up to use as cigarette papers.

The Deserter

Hiding between a stone wall and a low shrub
he waits for the night.
For what he plans to do
is best done without light.
His rifle he has cast aside;
in a ditch it lies out of sight.
It is better to go empty-handed.
It is dangerous enough to cross over
to the enemy lines unarmed;
carrying a weapon
could easily give the wrong impression
and he wants to arrive unharmed.
He sits huddled in his bubble of fear.
He is doubly afraid:
his former friends are now his foes
and his erstwhile foes are not yet his friends.
One dominant thought spurs him on –
soon, if fortune favours him, he will
be with his parents in Seville.

Chapter 15 : The defence of Hill 666
7-29 August 1938

In the early hours of 7th August, after thirteen days of continuous front-line action, the 15th Brigade went to the rear, and for
ten days we could rest, read our mail, write home and try to get
rid of the vermin with which we were infested.

It was at this time that I first heard a song that would be
recorded some twenty years later by Pete Seeger. It was a warm,
still evening and I was lying on my blankets under a tree when,
out of the silence, I heard a plaintive tenor voice:

> *Si me quieres escribir*
> *Ya sabes mi paradero,*
> *En el frente de Gandesa,*
> *Primera línea de fuego.*
> (If you want to write to me
> You know where I am,
> On the Gandesa front,
> In the firing line.)

We were encamped in a large field dotted with hazelnut trees
not far from the Ebro. Here we were not bothered by enemy
aircraft, though reconnaissance planes flew over frequently. The
cookhouse staff were able to give us hot meals, and we had an
issue of cigarettes and were given our arrears of pay. Actually I
had plenty of cigarettes, as among my mail were five copies of the
News Chronicle and three copies of the local newspaper, the
Wallasey and Wirral Chronicle, which my father had sent me.
Inside each newspaper were ten cigarettes.

In the machine gun company there was a tall, good-looking
New Zealander named Van Orren, whose real name was
Vaughan. A good many Americans and Canadians, too, went to
Spain under assumed names, to avoid, perhaps, political
persecution on their return. Van Orren had not lived in New
Zealand for some time because, before going to Spain, he had

served in the Household Cavalry.[53]

One day, when I was lazing under an olive tree, having treated myself to the luxury of a wash and shave, a delousing session and half an hour of letter-writing, Van Orren came over to me and said: 'I'm going shopping. Are you coming along?' I noticed that he, a non-smoker, had an unopened packet of Camel. I had a tablet of soap and some razor-blades. We set off down the road in the direction of the Ebro. Republican artillery was firing over our rest area to pound the enemy lines, which were not far away. We soon reached a farmhouse.

I explained to the farmer's wife that we wanted to buy fruit but she was not at all keen to accept Republican bank-notes. There was nowhere, she explained, where she could spend them. When we produced the soap, the cigarettes and the razor-blades, her attitude changed completely. In less than five minutes, Van Orren's rucksack was filled with peaches, grapes, melons and figs. She then produced a dozen eggs.

'No,' I said, and explained that we had no means of cooking them. In the end she made us sit down at the kitchen table and we each had three fried eggs. We took the other half-dozen back with us, hard-boiled.

One day the battalion postman called to me. 'There's a large parcel here for you, comrade.' I looked at the writing and, seeing that the parcel was from my mother, realised that it had been sent as a birthday present, my twenty-second birthday being on 24th August. I opened the parcel and found that it contained a large fruit-cake. It must have weighed about five pounds. Unfortunately it had been in transit for a long time and one side of it was green with mould.

'You can't eat that, it's mouldy. If you do, you'll be ill,' said Tom Murray.

'I'll throw the green part away,' I replied. 'The rest of it looks okay.' Tom still looked dubious. That night we heard that we were to go back to the front. I didn't want to be encumbered by the heavy cake so I ate the 'good' part, with the help of two or three friends.

On 17th August we marched back towards Gandesa, but this time not to the Sierra de Caballs, where we had failed to take Hill

481. Instead we scrambled up the goat-tracks of the Sierra de Pandols. The 15th Brigade did not go into action immediately. We were held in reserve, but we dug in, for the Fascist bombers were constantly overhead. Now we saw nothing of the Republican Air Force. Maybe all our planes had been shot down. At any rate, the fascists had undisputed air supremacy.

The day before my twenty-second birthday we moved into front-line positions, high up in the sierra. On our right flank was a Spanish unit and on two or three occasions I was called upon to act as interpreter when Sam Wild and Bob Cooney conferred with Spanish officers. We would lie on our stomachs behind a low parapet of jagged rocks, while they exchanged opinions and instructions. We could see Gandesa quite clearly, and the road at the back of the town along which the enemy brought up their supplies. We could see their trucks, like Dinky toys, and the troops, like tiny puppets. All the time we were being shelled and their whine was mixed with the screech of rifle and machine gun bullets and the even more frightening sound of ricochets.

This time our task was to defend Hill 666, a mountain of blue-grey slate. It sloped gradually to a ridge, where we established our machine gun posts. There was hardly any cover – nothing but a few shattered tree-stumps and the burnt and blasted remains of bushes. Daily the enemy launched attacks against this hill. The capture of it would relieve the pressure on Gandesa. Every day the fascists shelled and bombed our positions; every night we rebuilt our gun emplacements, ate the food that was brought in huge metal containers and waited for the next day's attack.

Besides the bullets, bombs and shells, our greatest worry was water, or the lack of it. We were fighting some two thousand feet above sea-level in rugged terrain, and all water had to be transported up narrow tracks on the backs of mules. Consequently, in front-line positions there was never enough water to quench our thirst, while washing or even shaving was out of the question. There was an hour's respite after the breakfast coffee, when the air was still relatively cool. But when the heavy fighting resumed, as it usually did about 9am, and the merciless sun had climbed so high as to eliminate any shade, our mouths became dry and our tongues swollen. In this dehydrated state our voices sounded cracked and we talked as little as possible.

In the machine gun company we were even worse off. The old Maxims were water-cooled. If they dried out they seized up, so the guns always had priority. If we had a ration of *vino tinto* with a meal, we used to save it in our water-bottles, and on one occasion we even had to sacrifice our wine and use it as a coolant. Others urinated in order to provide the necessary liquid. We spoke little and most of us took refuge in sleep. I found that I could sleep anywhere, in any position, at any time of the day or night during a lull in the fighting.

Although we had enough ammunition, we had hardly any equipment. Most of us were bare-headed, dressed in shirts and trousers. Few had boots. Most of us wore sandals or rope-soled *alpargatas*. I doubt if there were more than four steel helmets in the whole company. We had no pouches, but carried our ammunition in our pockets or in bags tied to our belt.

Flies, too, added to our discomfort. There were millions of them, attracted, I suppose, by the stench of blood and putrefaction which hung over the whole area. This was inevitable when the dead often lay for days in the hot summer sun before they could be buried, and even then had to be placed in very shallow graves. Deep graves could not be dug in that rocky terrain.

Then, of course, we were lousy. It was impossible to avoid becoming infested with lice. Like all the others I could neither wash nor shave and my tattered uniform was stained black in places where blood had dried on it. There were all kinds of 'remedies' advocated. Some said that Spanish brandy would kill lice, but who would waste brandy on vermin? Others recommended vinegar (but we hadn't any). Some men would undress completely and run the hems of their clothes over a flame in an attempt to kill the creatures. But it was a losing battle. A Scotsman said to me once: 'Ye canna say ye're really lousy until ye can put your hand inside your shirt and pick a big yin from amang the wee yins.'

We suffered heavy casualties, many comrades being killed, or wounded so badly that they had to be taken to hospital. Most of us had bandages covering small flesh wounds. But there was no let-up in the battle. The Caproni bombers seemed to be above us all the time, though they concentrated their attention on our lines of communication in the valley below. Their bombing was inaccurate and I suppose because we were so near the fascist front line the Italians were afraid of hitting their side. The shelling continued, however.

From his notebook in Spain, the author's list of the machine gun company personnel, indicating whether they were killed (k), wounded (w), sick (s), executed (ex) or taken prisoner (p) in the Battle of the Ebro.

A few days before my birthday, George Jackson was killed. I was greatly saddened. The coal-miner from Cowdenbeath had been a particular friend of mine, despite our different ages and backgrounds.54 It was in this battle, too, that one of our company went 'off his head'. I had been told by Tom Murray to go and let the gun crew leaders know it was time to send men to the rear to fetch the supper, which had just arrived. As I made my way up the slope towards the machine gun positions I met this comrade wandering aimlessly on the hill. I tried to persuade him to go to the rear, but soon found that it was quite useless talking to him in his shell-shocked condition. He repeatedly told me that George Jackson was still alive, even though I knew perfectly well that George was dead.

'I tell you he's alive. He's just given me a roll of tobacco.' This was his parting remark as I left to deliver the message to the gun crews.

* * * * *

At midnight on 28th August we were relieved by a Spanish unit. We slipped and scrambled down the track and then, in fours, marched along the road to an orchard where there was plenty of cover. I tried to sleep, but had a very bad night and the first thing I did, on waking, was vomit. I was unsteady on my feet and wondered what was wrong with me. I tried to take down some breakfast but vomited again immediately. I was also suffering from diarrhoea. Tom Murray advised me to report sick and I decided to do so if I was no better next day. I ate nothing all day, hoping that the sickness would pass, but I had another sleepless night.

I reported to the battalion medical post, and was sent to the brigade medical officer. The doctor, who had an American accent, did not say much, but he looked carefully into my eyes, pulling down the lower lids. Then he felt my abdomen and said that I would have to go to hospital.

'Why?' I answered. 'I've only got guts-ache. Can't you give me something to settle it?'

'You have more than an upset stomach,' he replied. 'I'd bet a month's pay that you have yellow jaundice. I'm going to send you to hospital, so I advise you to have a wash.'

I must have been a sight. I had neither washed nor shaved for more than a week and my hair was long and unkempt. My clothes were filthy and blood-stained; my toes were sticking out of my shoes.

If You Had Lived

In memory of my friend George Jackson of Cowdenbeath,
killed by a fascist bullet near Gandesa, August 1938.

If you had lived
I should not be thinking of you now.
Our friendship would have ended
with the de-lousing treatment,
the day we took off our tattered uniform,
handed in our obsolete rifles and,
giggling like children,
donned the Cagney hats
and the ill-fitting suits
that a grateful government gave us.
But you were not demobbed, Geordie.
A round hole
explosively dug by a fascist shell
is your grave in the high sierra.
Stark, burnt tree-trunks
were watchful mourners
as we laid you, coffinless,
in the Spanish earth you went to defend.
Death's finger-print was on your forehead –
a small round spot
like a caste-mark.
Your grave is unmarked,
un-numbered,
unregistered
but now the sweet thyme of peace sheds its perfume
over the place where you lie.
If you had lived, Geordie,
I should not be thinking of you now.
Our front-line friendship
would have ended
with a handclasp and 'Good luck!'
We would have gone our separate ways,

you back to the blackness of the pit
and I to an office desk,
but the bullet that ended your life
soldered and eternalised our friendship.
Every August I think of you, Geordie.

Chapter 16 : In hospital
30 August-23 September 1938

I walked back to the machine gun company HQ feeling very ill indeed. I collected my haversack containing my few personal possessions and then reported to Tom Murray that I was being sent to hospital. I think he was genuinely sorry to see me go. 'I shall miss you,' he said. 'I don't know how I shall manage without an interpreter.'

Rafael Garmendia came part of the way to the medical post, and shook hands with me, after we had exchanged home addresses. 'Just in case we don't meet up again,' he said. I waited for nearly two hours with half-a-dozen other men, some of whom were wounded.

Eventually, on 30th August, I recrossed the Ebro, this time in a motor-launch, and was taken by ambulance to the hospital at Cambrils, arriving early in the afternoon.

In the hospital we were offered food and drink and, as I felt a little better, I thought I ought to try and eat something, if only to keep up my strength. I had no appetite, but forced down a few mouthfuls. I immediately felt sick again. The only receptacle near at hand was a large brass flower-pot container. Luckily there was no flower-pot in it, so I vomited into it.

A nurse ran up, thanked me for not being sick all over the polished floor and took me straight to see a doctor. He was an elderly, bespectacled man, on whom the military uniform seemed out of place. He examined me and told the nurse that I would have to be sent on the following day to another hospital further from the front.

I was taken, again by ambulance, to La Sabinesa hospital just outside Tarragona. There I had a hot bath and was able to shave. My filthy clothes were taken away and I was given a pair of pyjamas and put to bed. The luxury of lying on a soft mattress and between cool sheets, for the first time in months, was quite indescribable and I felt happy and ill at the same time.

I was rather mystified by the attitude of the nurses, however.

They were curt, to the point of rudeness, and seemed unwilling to talk to me. When I asked one of them for a glass of water, I received the answer: 'Yes, if I have time.'

Next morning this particular nurse came to my bedside and apologised for her rudeness of the previous night. 'I'm afraid the documents which came with you got mixed up and we mistook you for another soldier who has venereal disease.'

A Spanish doctor examined me. At first he said nothing, but when he found that I spoke Spanish he confirmed that I had yellow jaundice. He added that I was in very poor condition and would be out of the war for some time. He said that he would make arrangements for me to be transferred next day to the International Brigades' hospital near Gerona.

Still wearing pyjamas – I had no other clothes – I was taken in an ambulance to the railway station and transferred to a hospital train which left Tarragona in the late afternoon. I felt sick and took little interest in the journey.

It must have been two or three o'clock in the morning of 2nd September when I was taken from the train and, in an ambulance, finally reached Farnés de la Selva (previously called Santa Coloma de Farnés), where the International Brigades had a hospital. I was helped up to the first floor to a room containing three beds, two of which were unoccupied. After the orderly had left, I introduced myself to my room-mate, who had been wakened by the noise. He was a Spaniard whose home was in Sao Paulo, Brazil. He had returned to Spain to fight against Franco. He informed me that he was an epileptic, and explained what I was to do if he had an attack. He added that he was glad to have some company.

At about nine o'clock a Spanish woman doctor and a Spanish nurse came to see me. After giving me a thorough examination, the doctor prescribed the medicine I was to have, and told the nurse that I was to be put on a 'C diet'. This, the nurse informed me later, meant that I was to have no eggs, no meat, no fruit, no vegetables, but plenty of milk.

She told me that her name was España.

'A strange name,' I said.

'My father was an anarchist,' she explained, 'and refused to give me the name of a Christian saint.'

One of the kindest nurses was Susi Velasco, from Barcelona. She was only about four and a half feet tall and was always active. However, no matter how busy she was, she always found time for a joke with the patients. Later I met other nurses – most of them Spanish, but there were a few 'Internationals'. One of these was Florence Pike, whose home was in Paris, Ontario.[55] Whenever I received tea from my mother, she could be persuaded to 'brew-up' over a Bunsen burner. In fact our tea-parties became quite famous and often attracted six or more British comrades.

On the first day of my stay in hospital, there was a knock at my door and in walked Dave Newman, whom I had not seen since my days in the Tarazona office. He was recovering from typhoid. He used to visit me every day, and we often spent hours chatting. He would bring me books from the hospital library and Spanish newspapers. Dave, too, helped me to spend my pay, buying for me notepaper, envelopes and razor-blades from the hospital shop.

He told me that the hospital was a converted hotel, and that before the war it had been patronised by wealthy people who came to drink the mineral waters, for which Farnés was famous.

During the first four or five days I felt really ill and sometimes even Dave Newman's visits were irksome. Then the sick feeling left me, but I was still not allowed out of bed for another couple of weeks. As my diet was so restricted, I existed on bread and sweetened milk.

I must have been in very poor physical condition indeed because if I banged or scratched myself enough to break the skin, the wound, no matter how insignificant, refused to heal. This happened one night when, not wishing to bother the night-nurses, I got out of bed and tottered the twenty yards along the corridor to the lavatory. On returning to my room, I knocked my knee on the corner of an iron bedstead. Two days later I could hardly move my leg and there was a large, suppurating sore where I had broken the skin.

On another occasion I scratched the back of my hand, with the same result. For weeks I went about with a bandaged hand, gaining undeserved sympathy from people who thought I had

149

been wounded in battle.

* * * * *

From time to time other sick or wounded soldiers of the British Battalion were admitted to the hospital. Dave used to make a point of visiting newcomers, and he often used to bring me interesting items of news, gossip or rumour. It was from him that I first learned of the massive counter-offensive that the fascists had mounted. They obviously wanted to reconquer as soon as possible the land we had liberated in a day and a half some two months previously. There had been no indication in the Spanish newspapers of the extreme gravity of the military situation. The enemy had numerical superiority in men, munitions and, most important of all, aircraft, and the Spanish People's Army was being forced to give ground.

I also received news of some of my friends at the front. I learned, for example, that Rafael Garmendia, who had so often made us laugh, had been killed, as well as Jack Nalty and Bill McGregor, who had taken command of our company after Paddy Duff had been wounded.[56]

Early in September one of the English comrades came to see me. 'So, you're a bloody hero, eh?' he said.

The expression on my face must have indicated that I did not know what he was talking about.

'You've been mentioned in dispatches for bravery,' he explained.

'What the hell are you talking about?' I thought it must be some kind of joke.

'Haven't you seen any of the English papers that came today?'

'No.'

'Wait a bit then, comrade.'

He left the room and returned a few minutes later with a copy of the *Daily Worker*, which he put into my hands. On an inside page there was a list of British volunteers who had been mentioned in dispatches. I saw the names of a number of my comrades – Jack Nalty, Paddy Duff, George Jackson, John Smith and others. At the foot of the list I read my own citation:

Private JR Jump (company secretary) for having fulfilled his duty, especially as an interpreter, without faltering in a number of meetings held under intense enemy fire.[57]

My mind went back to Hill 666 and the interpreting I had done for Jack Nalty when, lying on our stomachs, we had gazed down on Gandesa while the shells had whistled overhead. Little had I guessed, when Tom Murray showed me the citations he had written, that he had intended to add my name to the list.

* * * * *

On 9th September there was a fiesta in Farnés, to which many of the patients went, but I was still not allowed out of bed. When Susi Velasco came in with a bowl of water for me to have a wash, she suggested that I should have a shave too.

'I shaved yesterday,' I replied.

'But you must make yourself handsome,' she said. 'You're going to have visitors.'

'Visitors?'

'Yes, some pretty girls.'

During the morning a group of five or six young ladies came into my room with España. They were visiting all the bed-patients in the hospital. After they had asked me where I was from and why I was in hospital, they presented me with four enormous peaches.

'*Muchas gracias.*' I said, 'but I cannot eat them, as I'm on a very strict diet. I must not eat fruit.'

'Could he eat them if they were stewed?' one of the girls asked España.

'I think so. I'll ask the doctor.'

The doctor must have given permission, for España took the peaches to the kitchen. That evening I had an extra treat for supper, stewed peaches.

While I was in hospital my mail arrived more regularly than at any other time in Spain and I received more letters because, having plenty of time on my hands, I wrote to all my relatives and to my former colleagues on the *Worthing Herald*.

Gradually I recovered my strength. The yellowness faded from my chest and face, which I examined every morning when I went to the lavatory. Finally only the yellowness of the whites of my eyes showed the symptoms of jaundice. At last, after close on three weeks in bed, I was given a thorough medical examination by a German woman doctor who pronounced me fit to get up and to go on to a 'B diet'. This meant that I could have anything except fresh fruit and fresh vegetables and, most important of all, I would eat in the dining-hall. The doctor seemed more concerned with the sores on my hand and leg, and told me that I was still a long way from being fit.

Each morning orderlies visited the patients and gave us our diet-tickets for the day – blue for 'C diet', pink for 'B diet' and white for 'A diet'. The 'B diet' had printed on it in Spanish: Breakfast – Milk – Lunch – Milk – Dinner. As I received my tray of food or bowl of warm milk, the ticket was punched against the appropriate item. 'A diet' patients had no milk between meals.

We ate in fours at tables placed in the dining-hall, which served as a lounge and reading-room between meals. There, we could write letters, read, play chess, draughts and cards and listen to the radio.

There was a loud-speaker on the wall, so that we were kept up-to-date with the news. Although the official war communiqués always tried to hide the bad news, it was clear that things were not going well on the Ebro front.

Besides the news reports and the pep-talks (and it was often difficult to distinguish between the two) the radio programmes consisted almost entirely of recorded music – military marches, Spanish folk-music and Ravel's 'Boléro'. This last record was played so often – six or seven times a day – that a point was reached when, as soon as the first notes came over the air, there would be the chorus of protests, groans and laughter.

'Oh Christ, not again!'

'Is that the only goddam record they have?'

'I wish someone would smash the bloody thing!'

'If that happened the station would have to close down.'

We talked a lot about food, the food we had been deprived of in Spain. I remember thinking longingly of bread and butter and of tea with milk.

Miles Tomalin, the writer and poet, never tired of talking about food and drink and one day we had a discussion to decide what particular item of food was most typically British. In turn we rejected fish and chips, sausage and mash, pancakes with lemon and sugar and even plum-pudding. We finally agreed that the most typical of all British foods was baked jam roll. 'When we get back to England,' said Miles, 'let's found a Baked Jam Roll Club, for the defence of the good old British pudding.'

'We could call it simply the Pudding Club,' I suggested, at which he threw a book at my head.

* * * * *

During September there had been growing rumours that the Spanish government intended to dispense with the services of all foreign volunteers. Our numbers had decreased as a result of the recent fighting, and the flow of new volunteers had stopped some months previously. Most of the officers and men in the International Brigades were now Spaniards.

These rumours became stronger and stronger until, on 21st September, we heard on the radio that the prime minister, Dr Juan Negrín, had announced to the League of Nations in Geneva that the Republic had decided to repatriate all foreign troops, even those who had acquired Spanish nationality since the start of the war.

Could this be true? Even now we found it hard to believe, but next morning the daily papers carried confirmation and stated that the League of Nations itself was going to supervise the withdrawal and repatriation of the Internationals.[58] Why had the Spanish government taken this decision? Some said it was to shame Franco into following suit and sending home his German and Italian troops. The 'official line' was that the Spanish People's Army was now strong enough to fight alone without foreigners. I thought that the government's decision was simply an act of compassion. The leaders knew that the war was lost and

153

that if we were captured we would almost certainly be shot. Therefore they decided to send us home where, at least, we would be useful propagandists against fascism.

Once we had seen the news in black and white we believed it, and from that moment we all started thinking and talking about our families and homes, our jobs and what we intended to do on our return. The big question in everybody's mind was: 'When?'

If You Had Seen

If you had seen the things I've seen,
you, breakfast-table readers of the Peerage Press,
If you, stolid tube-train drinkers
of a crazed lord's bath-water,
had lain on your swollen stomachs in the mud
while the shadow of the 'planes passed over.
If you had fallen to the ground
hunting for cover where there was none
as bullets whipped the grass above your head,
you would not think about the Spanish War
solely in gilded terms of Stock Exchange.

If you, drab wives of smug suburban husbands,
had felt what I have felt
watching
motor-truck loads of frightened tear-eyed children
transported from war to peace
from parents' love to strange nurses' care;
if you had seen
thin legs and pale faces of milk-needy children,
hospitals without eggs
where nurses wash sheets without soap;
if you had seen boy soldiers marching on bare, cut feet;
if you had seen houses (and remember homes)
smashed by bombs from Holy Roman 'planes,
you would not say:
'I'm glad it's Spain, not here' and change the subject.

If you, grovelling worshippers of the great God Garvin,
had seen a 'dud' aerial torpedo
three feet long, and
with German eagle markings;
if you (like I) had questioned
Italian Air Force pilots,

seen new Caproni bombers,
German canon, Fiat automatics,
you would not hold your tongues!
You would shout with us, 'The Pyrenees are down!'
A bolted door cannot keep out a plague.
A wordy protest will not stop a lion.
And charity must never stay at home.

Santa Coloma de Farnés, 6th September 1938

Chapter 17 : Waiting to be demobbed
23 September-25 November 1938

Soon after we learned that we were to be repatriated and the International Brigades disbanded, I began to detect a quite noticeable change in our attitudes and behaviour. Up to that point the future seemed the same for all of us. As soon as we were fit for front line service we would be posted back to our units. There we would be re-infested with lice, eat at irregular times and go for days without washing and shaving, while attacking Hill This or defending Hill That.

In such circumstances we had been absolutely united, and, if any of us had been asked when we would return to our mother countries, we would have replied: 'When we have won the war.' Cut off, as we were, from news, other than those propagating the 'official line', we still imagined that, if we fought against the dictators long enough, pressure of public opinion would force the democracies to abandon their policy of appeasement.

Now we faced the prospect of returning to our homes, and slowly, almost imperceptibly, this unity began to evaporate. We did not quarrel. We were still comrades, but something had suddenly come between us. Elias Schultz was a New Yorker and would return to the Bronx; I was English and would be sent back to Wallasey. The Spaniards, poor fellows, would stay and carry on fighting the war which they were told they would eventually win.

We began to associate more and more in national groups. We talked of our homes, our families, our ambitions and plans for the future, and this produced a further weakening of our unity. The intellectuals and the manual workers, who hitherto had been united in a single cause, now found that they had little in common.

Dave Newman and I were together most of the time. We wandered about the hospital grounds. The weather was still very warm and we did a lot of sunbathing. We tried to identify the different trees and shrubs. We watched the behaviour of ants. We read most of the English books in the hospital library. We talked of the future, and of the civil war.

'Well, it's not because they can win the war without us,' said Dave.

'Certainly not. They can't win it with us,' I put in.

'Perhaps they think we shall be such great propagandists when we get back, that we shall swing the public opinion against the policy of non-intervention.'

'Well, as a fighting force we don't count for much. Less than a quarter of the International Brigades are foreigners.'

During the last week of September some British and American wounded were brought to the hospital, and from them we learned of the fierce battles that had raged right up to 23rd September when the International Brigades were finally taken out of the front line for the last time.

Under the relentless bombing and artillery fire, the 15th Brigade had been gradually forced back, retreating from one ridge to another, fighting all the way. Jack Nalty had returned from hospital and resumed command of my old company, only to be killed on the very last day.[59]

My letters home changed. Previously, because of the strict censorship, they had merely consisted of 'I'm all right' and 'How are you?' Occasionally I described some non-military incident, or commented on some political event in the world outside Spain, but I could never tell those at home where I was, where I had been nor what I was doing. Now, I could tell my parents, my brother Jack and my fiancée Cayetana that I was in hospital recovering from jaundice and that I expected to be home very soon. We really thought that repatriation would take only a few weeks.

Suddenly I had a longing for all those little luxuries of home which my sub-conscious mind had suppressed while I knew they were unobtainable. I thought of buttered toast, fish and chips, plates of sausage, mash and fried onions, and pints of beer.

From 15th to 17th October there was a weekend of fiestas in Farnés, organised by the Socorro Rojo Internacional in honour of the International Brigades, including film shows and dances. The hospital lounge was decorated for a dance on the Saturday evening. Political slogans and flags of all nations were hung on the walls. The dance seemed to attract all the pretty girls of the district. It was good to have some feminine company, though I was not much of a dancer and the dances were strange ones – *pasodobles*, *sardanas* and *jotas*.

* * * * *

One day we read in *Frente Rojo* that the League of Nations commission which had been set up to supervise the counting and withdrawal of foreign volunteers had arrived in Spain. Shortly afterwards the hospital was visited by a group of officers, and the English-speaking volunteers were interviewed. One by one we were ushered into the presence of a kindly Royal Navy officer.

When I went in he told me to sit down and he asked me my full name. I told him.

'Where and when were you born?'

I gave him the information he asked for, my father's full name and address.

'We need this information just to make sure that you are a British subject,' he explained. 'Have you been wounded?' he asked, looking at the bandaged hand.

'No, I've had jaundice and they tell me that my blood is out of condition. I keep coming out in sores.'

'Are you being well looked after?'

'Yes, the staff here are really wonderful.'

He smiled at me, rather as a father might smile at a naughty child who was suffering as a result of its disobedience.

'When are we likely to return home?' I asked him.

'These things take time. You know what the red tape is, I suppose,' he said. 'We'll have you out as soon as possible, but you mustn't complain. You got yourself into this mess, you know.'

The interviews took the whole of one day. When the officers had departed, we all felt that things were moving at last. It was noticeable that the foreign volunteers started to be more careful with their money, spending it only on articles that would be useful on their return or during the journey. Some bought suitcases, others clothing, wallets and cigarette cases.

The weather was fine and warm and Dave Newman and I used to spend hours in the uncared for hospital grounds reading. I read Margaret Landon's *Anna and the King of Siam*, Ralph Fox's *Genghis Khan* and a number of novels by Sinclair Lewis. When there were no other English books we had not read, we even turned to the Bible.

One day Dave found a chestnut tree beneath which there were hundreds of fat chestnuts on the grass. We went there, made a fire and roasted chestnuts on a piece of scrap metal that was on a rubbish dump. It helped to pass the time.

I had regained my strength and was put on an 'A diet'. I wrote to my mother and, in answer to my request, she sent me some Oxo cubes. At mealtimes we sat four to a table and I generally ate with Bill Harrington, Miles Tomalin and Dave Newman. We were the recipients of envious looks and scrounging pleas from others when, having been given our soup, we would cut an Oxo cube into four and thus add some flavour to a watery soup.

The main course was nearly always some kind of stew with beans, chickpeas, lentils or potatoes. There were always some pieces of rather rubbery meat which seemed quite 'toothproof'. With a very sharp knife, it was, however, possible to cut the meat into thin slivers and swallow them.

We used to speculate about the animal that produced such unchewable meat. Miles suggested that it might be a newly-discovered creature called *Tyreus Dunlopidae Nonmasticabila*. Then, one day, I found out the truth. The meat was obviously donkey meat. How did I know, the others asked and I showed them the proof. I picked up a cube of meat from my plate and let them all see the unmistakably asinine grey fur attached to it.

* * * * *

In order to ensure that no fit men were kept too long in hospital, a medical commission used to visit hospitals regularly. Now, there was no question of our being sent to the front, but when the commission came at the end of October I wondered if I would be sent to rejoin the rest of the British while awaiting repatriation.

When I went in and sat down the staff doctor said that I was still not in good health and ought to stay longer in hospital. Dave Newman also got a 'reprieve'. I have no doubt that, were it not for the fact that the Spanish government had decided to fight the war without foreign volunteers, I would have been found *apto para el frente* (fit for front-line duty). I felt perfectly fit in every way.

Time passed slowly, and we began to wonder if we would still be in Spain for Christmas. To overcome the boredom I started writing letters to the correspondence columns of the *Wallasey and Wirral Chronicle*, a weekly newspaper on the staff of which I had served my apprenticeship as a reporter. There were always plenty of replies, for Franco had many vociferous supporters on Merseyside.

I received a letter from Fernando Sanz Compán, a Spanish newspaper correspondent in Liverpool. He had read my letters and wrote to thank me for what I had done for his country, he being much too old to fight. In his letter he compared the idealistic International Brigaders to Don Quijote, who did good without any thought of reward; Franco, the Nazis and the fascists he likened to the worldly, greedy Sancho Panza.

October ended and we were still waiting, each day more bored and impatient. I suppose that I was luckier than most because, having read all the English books in the hospital library, I could now read the Spanish ones and also the Spanish newspapers. Every day a number of copies of *Frente Rojo* and *La Vanguardia* were delivered to the hospital.

I read a very bad translation of an English book about Kaiser Wilhelm. It was such a bad translation as to be incomprehensible in parts. I recall one sentence: '*El Kaiser dijo a los aviadores que no bombardeasen a Miss Buckingham*'. After much thought it occurred to me that the original English sentence must have been 'The Kaiser told the airmen to miss Buckingham Palace.'

To go into Farnés one needed a pass, and there was always a Spanish sentry on the gate whose job it was to examine the passes. These were given out freely, but often there was no-one in the office who had the authority to issue one. I discovered, however, that some of the detachment of soldiers who guarded

Mugshot in the author's International Brigade personnel file.
Photo: RGASPI (Russian State Archive of Socio-Political History)
International Brigade Collection.

the hospital were illiterate. When they were on duty we found that any piece of paper would do – provided that it bore the impression of a rubber-stamp. I used to present the pistol permit I had been given in Tarazona, while Dave Newman used an old safe-conduct of mine.

In the end this became a kind of game – to see who could get past the sentry with the most unlikely-looking 'pass'. One patient claimed that he had on one occasion got out with a piece of newspaper bearing a rubber-stamp, but nobody believed him. The sentries might be illiterate, but they were no fools and could distinguish typing from printing.

With Dave Newman and a Canadian I strolled the half mile to Farnés. There was nothing to do there except drink wine in one of the bars. Most of the shops had completely empty shelves.

Many had cards in the windows announcing which commodities were unavailable, 'No hay patatas' (no potatoes), 'No hay tabaco' (no tobacco), 'No hay jabón' (no soap) etc; on the door of one little shop there was a piece of paper with the words 'No hay nada' (there's nothing). I did manage, however, to buy a pair of socks and some envelopes.

* * * * *

On 20th November there was another fiesta in Farnés, this time to say goodbye to the International Brigades and to commemorate the Catalan anarchist Buenaventura Durruti, who had been killed in November 1936. All the hospital patients who were well enough marched to Farnés, where the name of the main square was changed to Plaza de las Heroicas Brigadas Internacionales (quite a mouthful!). During the afternoon there were football and basketball matches and in the evening a film show. We all interpreted this 'goodbye' as a sign that we would soon be on our way home, and our spirits rose.

As the nights grew longer and the days colder, we became more and more convinced that we would not be home for Christmas, nor even the new year. We became more irritable and occasionally quarrels broke out. All the Spaniards with whom I came into contact said they were sorry we were leaving, but I suspected that in their hearts they were glad. It was, after all, their war and no-one is more patriotic than a Spaniard. Perhaps many of them felt that without so many foreigners on their soil it might be easier for the Republic to obtain some kind of peace with honour.

Suddenly, without any warning at all, on 25th November, it was announced that we were to leave the hospital that very day. We would depart, in fact, as soon as army lorries came to take us on the first stage of our journey home.

As the doctors considered that I was still not fully recovered, I was discharged from the Spanish People's Army on medical grounds and was given an impressive document signed by the under-secretary for the army. This stated that, having sacrificed my health in the service of the Republic, I was entitled to share

163

the fruits of victory. I was also given a card bearing the text, in Spanish, English and French, of the speech made by Dolores Ibárruri, on the occasion of the International Brigades' farewell march-past in Barcelona on 28th October: *Mothers! Women! When the years pass by and the wounds of the war are being staunched; when the cloudy memory of the sorrowful, bloody days returns in a present of freedom, peace and well-being; when the feelings of rancour are dying away and when pride in a free country is felt equally by all Spaniards, then speak to your children. Tell them of these men of the International Brigades.*

We were told to pack our belongings and be ready to leave within an hour. Packing my few things took no more than a few minutes, after which I wandered round the hospital to say goodbye to the doctors and nurses. Susi Velasco and España were both in tears as I kissed them goodbye and thanked them for all their kindnesses.

They were still weeping as they stood at the main door of the hospital and the lorries containing all the Internationals, except a few who were too ill to move, drove off. Clenched fists were raised and the shouting continued long after we were out of earshot.

'*¡Adiós y gracias!*'
'*¡Salud y victoria!*'
'*¡Viva la República!*'

Another Death

Another friend has died
and there is one more hole
in the wall of comradeship
erected over the years.
Time's insistent tide
washes its base
and many stones are loosened.
These are the friends I lose
to hospitals, nursing-homes,
far-off sheltered accommodation
and the reluctant love of distant daughters-in-law.
Occasionally a stone is washed away.
Then I attend a funeral
or a cremation.
A tricolour covers the coffin –
purple, yellow and red –
and I sit behind red-eyed family mourners who think they will
never forget.

I sigh,
return home
and, when I remember,
cross another name
out of my address-book.

Chapter 18 : Journey home
25 November-8 December 1938

We sang, cheered, laughed and shouted all the way along the main road to Barcelona, where we were taken to Las Planas on top of a hill overlooking the city. There, we were accommodated in a transit camp in which most of the troops were Spaniards. Our arrival came as a shock to the camp commandant, and he was certainly a bit of a shock to us.

We had been in the thick of the fighting and knew that our discipline was good, despite the fact that we addressed our NCOs and officers as 'comrade' (unless we knew their first names) and seldom saluted officers, most of whom chose not to wear badges of rank anyway. Here, in the transit camp, we found we were being ordered about by an immaculately uniformed captain who wore white gloves and who clearly believed in 'spit and polish'. He winced when we called him '*camarada*' and used the familiar '*tú*' form of address. When we discovered that our rations had been reduced on his authority, without our being informed, resulting in a whole day without any bread, we protested to him as a body. We must have seemed a rebellious rabble to him. We didn't stand to attention, nor call him '*señor*' or '*mi capitán*' as the Spanish conscripts did.

I was one of the spokesmen, and I asked him why we had been given no bread with our coffee.

'The men decided three weeks ago that they would go without bread one day a week, to help the war effort,' the camp commandant said.

'But as this is a transit camp, the men who took that decision are no longer here.'

'I am sorry, but there is nothing I can do about it.' He tried to walk away but we surrounded him.

'Don't you think you could have some special arrangements for us? We've had nothing to eat since midday yesterday except a bowl of stew.'

'There is nothing I can do about it. I have to make the same sacrifice myself.'

'We are as willing to make sacrifices as any Spaniards,' I answered, 'but we like to be consulted first.'

He did not reply but tried, again unsuccessfully, to walk back into his office.

'Why not give us half-rations for two days? We're hungry.'

At this he began to lose his temper. 'That would not be possible. We cannot alter the rules for you. You are soldiers and are subject to military discipline, or you ought to be. Now, I have other duties. I'm busy.'

We realised that we were up against a brick wall. He walked away. We sat down in front of his office and held a meeting to discuss our next move and decided to go to the HQ of the International Brigades in Barcelona. We did not go like a rabble, but formed up in fours and marched smartly out of the camp. The sentry presented arms as we went through the gate. Singing our favourite songs, we marched through the streets of Barcelona and halted outside the HQ, which was in a requisitioned house some distance from the city centre. A delegation of three went inside and came out shortly afterwards with a promise that we would stay in the transit camp no longer than was necessary. We must be patient. We would, our representatives told us, soon be rejoining our fellow countrymen, wherever they were.

As a number of us wanted to have a look at Barcelona, our officers dismissed us with instructions to make our way back to Las Planas.

'Let's see something of Barcelona,' Dave Newman suggested. 'If we have to go hungry, it will be more pleasant here than shut up in that camp.'

Barcelona was in a drab state, in spite of the multicoloured posters that adorned the walls of houses, shops and churches. Buildings looked dingy, their paintwork faded and peeling. Many had smashed windows patched up with plywood or cardboard. Most of the bars had little to offer by way of refreshment. There was plenty of fruit to be had. We bought oranges and grapes, but found nothing to satisfy our hunger pangs.

We returned to Las Planas by train. In the station there was a queue of at least forty people waiting to buy tickets. We took our

167

places at the end. A middle-aged woman turned round, on hearing our conversation.

'¿*Brigadas Internacionales*?' she asked.

'Yes, we are International Brigaders.'

'Then you must not wait here in the queue.' Raising her voice she addressed the others who were waiting to buy tickets. 'Let these young men go to the head of the queue. They are foreigners of the International Brigades. They should not have to stand here waiting.'

The others agreed and Dave and I found ourselves pushed to the front. Many patted us on the shoulder, and I heard one old man refer to us as heroes. 'Where are you going?' asked the man who was first in the queue.

'Las Planas.'

'Two tickets to Las Planas. I'll pay,' he told the booking-clerk, and handed over the money.

* * * * *

We spent three days in the transit camp outside Barcelona and at last, to our great joy, on 28th November we were taken in open lorries on a long drive northwards, until we reached Ripoll, a large town about twenty-five miles from the French frontier. It lies on the main railway line to Puigcerdá, near the eastern tip of Andorra.

The survivors of the British Battalion were billeted in an empty theatre, most of them sleeping in the aisles. Dave and I had to go up to the dress-circle to find a place where we could sleep.

Our arrival at Ripoll had all the characteristics of a homecoming and we spent the first day meeting old friends and exchanging news. I again met Sam Wild, Bob Cooney, Tom Murray, Joe Moran, Bill Harrington and Johnny Power, a cheerful little Irishman whom I had spoken to once or twice in the *barranco* at Marsá. All had harrowing stories to tell of the last terrible battles on 22nd and 23rd September, and of the wonderful reception they received from the people of Barcelona when they had taken part in the farewell march-past of the

International Brigades on 28th October.

Johnny Power had had all his teeth out, and I went with him to a dentist to see if he could be fitted with dentures.

'I've spent hardly any money since May,' he said, 'saving up to get some teeth.' The dentist took an impression of Johnny's gums and Johnny paid a deposit. On the way back, he told me two amusing anecdotes concerning his correspondence with his girlfriend in Ireland. They always wrote to each other in Gaelic and, when Johnny first arrived in Spain, this presented the censors with a headache, as there was no-one in the office who knew Gaelic. Finally, a letter was sent from the chief censor to his commanding officer asking whether Johnny was a trustworthy comrade. An affirmative reply was sent, and from that time his mail in Gaelic was stamped '*Visado por la censura*' (approved by the censor) without having been opened.

'Just take a look at this,' Johnny said to me, taking from the breast-pocket of his khaki shirt a soiled envelope. 'Examine it carefully.'

I did so. Addressed to Lieutenant John Power and posted in Waterford some five months earlier, the Irish post office had mis-sorted it and sent it to fascist Spain, where there was an Irish contingent who had volunteered to fight for Franco.

I examined all the rubber-stamp impressions and scribbled notes on the battered envelope, and it became clear that it had travelled to all parts of fascist Spain where any Irishman had ever been stationed. It had gone to hospitals, transit camps and training establishments. At last someone had guessed that the Irish post office had made a mistake, and wrote on the envelope '*probablemente España Roja*' (probably Red Spain). The letter was returned to Paris, and Johnny at last received it.

I have often thought about the dedicated Spanish post office worker. Ignoring the fact that a war was going on all around him, he still believed, like the Pony Express of the Wild West, that 'the mail must go through'.

* * * * *

The nights were cold in the Pyrenees, and I had no clothing

except what I stood up in, slacks, a cotton shirt and a pair of *alpargatas*. I went round all the shops trying to buy a pullover or jacket, but there was nothing of that kind to be had. Finally, I managed to buy a woollen scarf. It was about eight feet long and eighteen inches wide and had not been sold, I imagine, because of its colour. It was bright magenta. However, it helped to keep me warm, for it was long enough to go round my neck and also round my waist.

We were no longer organised in military companies, but in groups according to which part of the British Isles we came from. I could have joined the Merseyside group, but with Bill Harrington, Dave Newman and Miles Tomalin in the London and South-East England group, I joined that one, as I had been living in Worthing before joining up.

To keep us occupied the officers used to arrange marches in the morning – not route-marches with heavy loads that we had been used to. These were more like strolls, or social occasions. We would form fours and march three or four miles along the roads around Ripoll. The songs we sang this time were not only revolutionary songs and songs of battle, but songs from home. The marching-song of the London group was *Knocked 'Em in the Old Kent Road*. Other groups sang *Maggie May*, *Blaydon Races*, *Cwm Rhondda* or *Road to the Isles*. We also used to sing most of the bawdy songs which were to be sung in the Second World War and which had probably been sung by British soldiers since the days of Cromwell.

During the afternoons, when we were tired of strolling round the town, Dave Newman, Bill Harrington and I used to go into a café to sit down. The owner said he had no wine, no spirits, no beer. So we would pay a peseta for a siphon of soda-water and sit sipping that.

Dave and I had one great fear. We were terrified of becoming infested with lice again. Like all the others who had been in hospital we were free of body-lice, but we were sure that, in spite of baths, some of the others, who had come straight from the front, still had 'lodgers'. So we tended to keep to ourselves.

December came and we were still waiting. We became more and more bored and depressed. Every day there was a new rumour about our impending return, but no real facts. Nobody, in fact, really knew anything. Luckily the weather was dry. The days were warm, but at night it was bitterly cold. There were no air raids, and very few air-raid warnings. Had it not been for the shortages of almost all commodities and the large number of men in uniform, it would have been almost possible to forget about the war.

One Ripoll shopkeeper displayed great business enterprise in obtaining a supply of attractive-looking suitcases. As soon as I heard this I rushed to buy one for, though I had few articles of clothing, I had a number of books and a lot of papers – pamphlets, official documents and scraps of diaries. The case was of very poor quality, made of some kind of compressed cardboard, but it cost me one hundred pesetas. When I had packed it, I lifted it up to test the weight and the handle came off in my hand. I found a long piece of thick cord and tied it up.

Our last day in Spain was 6th December. At breakfast we were told that we would be leaving that day and must be packed up in half an hour's time. We were marched to a large hall where we were given civilian clothes – suit, shirt, underwear, socks and shoes – and we handed in our uniforms, except our berets which we were allowed to keep. I was given a light-grey summer suit. The trousers fitted me well enough but the jacket was voluminous, enough for two people of my size.

We were given time to spend any pesetas we had left. I bought another pair of *alpargatas* for twelve pesetas and a newspaper. There was little else worth buying in the shops. I had about six pesetas left, and I gave them to a little boy who was playing on the pavement. His face lit up and his eyes shone as he ran off clutching the money.

I met Johnny Power as I walked back to the theatre. 'Jesus! I thought I was going back to Ireland with a mouth full of new teeth, but I've just been to the dentist, and they're not ready yet. And I've lost the bloody deposit I paid the dentist.'

After lunch we were marched to the railway station where our cases were examined by customs officers. They were then locked up, to be collected later.

In the late afternoon we returned to the station and picked

171

up our luggage. It was growing dark as we climbed aboard the train, made up of goods wagons. Our last journey in Spain was to be like so many we had had when we were in uniform. On climbing into the wagon I slipped and fell, spraining my right ankle. It swelled so much that I took off my shoes and instead wore alpargatas. So my feet left Spain just as they had entered the year before.

The train pulled out of the station and slowly covered the twenty-five miles to Puigcerdá and the French frontier, where we were transferred into another train. There were dozens of police on the platform, presumably to see that we did not leave the train and try to return to Spain.[60]

When dawn came we were speeding towards Paris. The train came to a halt at a station and we were offered coffee and rolls by a group of Salvationists.

'Where was the Salvation Army when we were short of food in Spain?' someone shouted.

'We don't want your food. Send it to the children of Spain. They need it,' yelled another. Seeing that no-one was prepared to accept the food and drink offered, the Salvationists packed up their things and left. The train continued to wait, and we began to wonder what was going to happen.

Suddenly we heard the roar of a car-engine and a screech of brakes. A van marked 'Parti Communiste' had pulled up near the train. Some young men got out and started handing out cups of milky coffee and warm croissants. They also threw packets of Gauloises through the windows of the coaches. When we had finished breakfast, the train slowly pulled out of the station and we all sang *The Internationale*, those on the platform joining in.

I thought that we would have to change trains in Paris but, near the French capital, the train left the main line and, not long after, we passed through Versailles. So the French government was taking no chances with us. Perhaps they feared demonstrations against the policy of non-intervention.

The journey continued non-stop until we reached Dieppe in the mid-afternoon. We were given a meal on board the steamer. In Newhaven, as I limped towards the train, I heard a voice calling my name. It was Dorothy Thornycroft, who had driven over from Worthing to greet me.

* * * * *

It was dark on 8th December when we reached Victoria Station and in fours, with me limping because of my sore ankle, made our way through a bigger and more enthusiastic welcome than we could possibly have imagined. Johnny Power was by my side as we marched along a narrow path between pushing crowds on each side of the road. There were young men and girls, older men and women – some holding trade union or political party banners. All were cheering wildly. Packets of cigarettes were thrust into our hands; girls threw their arms round our necks and kissed us.

Suddenly I spotted a familiar face in the crowd. My brother Jack pushed his way to the front, came over to me and walked by my side. I noticed that he was wearing a black tie and was not smiling.

'I've come to tell you not to go back to Wallasey,' he said. 'There's no one there. Come to our flat in Manchester. Mother is with us. Father had a heart attack and died six days ago.'

I no longer saw the flags and banners. I no longer heard the cheering of the crowd, I seemed to be walking along in a bubble of silence, hearing only, over and over again, my brother's words: 'Father had a heart attack and died six days ago.'

Johnny Power, still walking at my side, had overhead everything. He put a sympathetic hand on my shoulder. 'I'm sorry, comrade,' he said. 'Tough luck.'

Lifelong Love

Long have I loved you.
In fifty years, my affection
has not altered
nor faltered.
My infatuation
has not lessened. It has not been
diluted by the rains of time
nor the tears of separation.
There have been bad moments,
painful periods when,
seeing you in the arms of my enemy,
I had to fight to
remain faithful in my love for you.
At last the nightmare ended.
You rejected my enemy
and became mine again –
a free and democratic Spain.

Afterword by Jim Jump:
James R Jump – A Spanish affair

My father was one of over two thousand Britons who enlisted in the International Brigades during the Spanish Civil War of 1936-39. Unlike nearly five hundred of them, he survived. This is his memoir, written in various stages from the 1960s onwards. Unpublished until now, *The Fighter Fell in Love* brings together two draft versions he produced, supplemented by elements of a diary he kept in Spain, plus some additional poems to the ones he selected.

As a budding *hispanista*, James arrived in Spain with a head start. Having learnt Spanish at Wallasey Grammar School, he was one of the few volunteers from Britain who could talk freely to Spaniards and indeed befriend them. He also had a Spanish fiancée waiting for him in England: Cayetana Lozano Díaz. She had arrived in Southampton on 23rd May 1937 as one of the *señoritas* looking after nearly four thousand refugee children escaping Hitler and Mussolini's terror bombing campaign in the Basque Country. James and Cayetana fell in love in the summer of 1937 while he was a volunteer at homes for the children in the Sussex coastal towns of Worthing and Lancing. They agreed to get married, but Cayetana, from San Sebastián, said she wanted to live in Spain, and James decided to join the International Brigades.

The memoir begins with James already determined to make the journey to Spain. In reality his journey had begun much earlier. Born on 24th August 1916 in Wallasey, then in Cheshire but now part of Merseyside, into a comfortably-off, politically Conservative family (his father owned a bakery), the author, like many of his generation growing up in the shadow of the First World War, was a pacifist and supporter of the Peace Pledge Union.[61] He was active too in his local St Thomas's Church and scripted a passion play, *Hail, Caesar*, about conflict between church and state. Though banned from being staged in the church itself by Bishop of Chester Geoffrey Fisher – a future

Archbishop of Canterbury – performances went ahead at Easter 1936 in the church hall.[62] From pacifism James gravitated towards socialism, especially under the influence of elder brother Jack, a student at Liverpool University.[63]

Anti-fascism and an interest in the Spanish Civil War developed in Worthing where, as a journalist, he was to report on the visits made by Haile Selassie to the seaside town. The exiled emperor's family stayed there while he travelled to and from Geneva to address the League of Nations in forlorn attempts to persuade member states to act decisively against Fascist Italy's invasion of Abyssinia.[64] Having learnt Spanish at school, James was already interested in the war in Spain. He recalls reading about the massacre of Spanish Republicans in the bullring at Badajoz in August 1936 and remembers Frank Cave, his editor at the *Worthing Herald,* knowing of this interest, passing him the news cables about the war.[65]

Then there was Cayetana. His bride-to-be and her sisters Antonia and Rosa were already refugees in Bilbao when in the spring of 1937 the Basque government asked for volunteers to help look after the 'children of Guernica' being evacuated to safety in Britain. The three sisters had escaped from San Sebastián before rebel soldiers entered the city in September 1936. Their brother, Policarpo, was meanwhile fighting in forces loyal to the Spanish Republic.

After a stormy passage through the Bay of Biscay the steamship *Habana* brought the three sisters and its cargo of *niños vascos* to Southampton. From a nearby holding camp outside Eastleigh, Cayetana was sent with a group of children along the coast to Worthing – where she met James.

Aged 22, she was a seamstress and ardent Republican supporter. Her political views and predicament no doubt made it easier for James to take the decision to go to Spain. He lost the war but won her hand and they were married in April 1940. Now with a British passport, Cayetana made two trips to Spain soon after the Second World War had ended to visit her mother in San Sebastián and to take messages to opponents of Franco's regime and food parcels to political prisoners.[66]

In Britain she also visited Spanish Republicans who had been slave labourers in the Nazi-occupied Channel Islands and who were now being interned in Adlington, Lancashire, alongside Axis prisoners. These men, she protested in letters to news-papers, had been 'conscripted against their will by the Germans', 'liberated' by the Allies and promptly 'put into British POW camps together with their former Gestapo and SS persecutors'.[67]

James and Cayetana with Basque children in Lancing, 1937.

Similarly, James continued campaigning following his return from Spain in December 1938 – when his memoir ends as abruptly as it starts. He addressed and chaired a series of meetings in Sussex, from Left Book Club, International Friendship League and Rotary Club branches to the 1939 Sussex congress of the Communist Party – of which he was a member – and Worthing's May Day rally. For a fortnight in March 1939 he ran a 'Spain Shop' and raised the equivalent of more than £600 for Spanish refugees in the south of France.[68] There were public meetings in Wallasey too, and even an article in his school old boys' magazine, in which he described the civil war as 'a phase in the struggle which has been going on for more than half a century for the emancipation of Spaniards'. His piece concluded: 'One thing is certain. The Spaniards have tasted liberty, they have been given a smattering of education. For a short time the Catalans and Basques have enjoyed living in "free states". And they will not forget it.'[69]

Why was Jump's memoir not published while the author was still alive? No correspondence or other clues are to be found in his papers, but I suspect that my father didn't try that hard. This would have been especially likely in the 1960s and 1970s, when interest in the International Brigades was relatively modest, though growing following the publication of Hugh Thomas's ground-breaking *The Spanish Civil War* in 1961 and then with the death of Franco in 1975.

James donated copies of a first draft to a number of archives,[70] and meanwhile delighted in the fact that his second-ary school Spanish language reader describing his participation in the Battle of the Ebro had been published in 1975.[71]

In the following year, the fortieth anniversary of the start of the civil war, Jump wrote a chapter in *The Distant Drum: Reflections on the Spanish Civil War* alongside contributions from other participants and eye-witnesses. Editor Philip Toynbee said: 'It is easily the best general picture of the International Brigade that I have had.'[72] In his review in the *New Statesman*, however, Oxford academic Valentine Cunningham, having judged that the two sides in the war 'enjoyed uncanny similarities', decided that Jump and fellow International Brigade veteran John Bassett 'reveal how decent men can commit themselves to an unthinkingly totalitarian inhumanity'.[73] Such was the prevailing Cold War-era orthodoxy, in which the elected government of the Spanish Republic and the rebel General Franco were seen as equivalents on left and right – a view demolished intellectually, if not wholly politically, in recent decades thanks to the work of historians in Britain and Spain.

During those lean postwar decades, James dedicated himself to writing about Spanish and Spain – as well as to raising a family and teaching in suburban Kent. The dust jacket of his first book, *The Spaniard and his Language*, announced in vague terms that the author had 'lived in Spain for some years'; presumably because admitting in 1951 that this period of time had been spent in the International Brigades would have been too much for anti-communist sensitivities.[74] Contrast this with *The Penguin Spanish Dictionary*, published in 1990, which boasted on its title page: 'As soon as he was twenty-one, [James R Jump] climbed over the Pyrenees, without a passport, to join the International Brigade in their fight against Franco, and was noted for bravery in despatches from the battle of the Ebro.'[75]

In the politically claustrophobic years of the Cold War Jump's internationalism found an unusual outlet in the world of Esperanto. He put the invented language on the curriculum at Temple School, Rochester, and in 1955, using contacts with Esperantists abroad, organised an international exhibition of children's art. The exhibition was an unexpected success, attracting entries from twenty-six countries, more than five thousand visitors and coverage on national TV news and in newspapers around the world. The opening ceremony saw the school choir sing in Esperanto, 'extolling the tremendous value of the common tongue, so that "nation shall speak peace unto nation".'[76]

Spanish, however, remained his first love, and the years until Franco's death in 1975 and the restoration of democracy saw James producing more than a dozen textbooks for students learning Spanish plus a steady stream of articles in language journals. Topics for the latter ranged from Spanish rugby terminology to modern Spanish nursery rhymes; from a history of Spanish grammars to Spain's changing imperative. Sometimes, inevitably, politics would intrude, especially on the subject of censorship. For example there was an article on the rehabilitation of Vicente Blasco Ibáñez, the novelist who died before the civil war yet whose work had been considered to be dangerously pro-Republican. Another reported on a visit in 1962 to Fuentevaqueros, birthplace and childhood home of Federico

García Lorca, murdered by the fascists in 1936. Older inhabitants still remembered him, but there was no mention or memorial in the village to Spain's greatest twentieth century poet and dramatist. A 1975 piece in the humorous weekly *El Cordoniz* described how it played cat-and-mouse with the censor. The magazine avoided direct political criticism of the Franco regime, but compensated for this by being outspoken on its administrative failures. It repeatedly demanded, for example, the publication of a secret report into the Matesa affair, a gigantic financial scandal exposed in 1970, involving prominent commercial and political figures.[77]

When Franco died in 1975 James and Cayetana decided to move to Spain. James gave up his teaching post at Medway and Maidstone College of Technology and in 1977 they settled in Logroño, capital of the northern region of La Rioja. These were momentous times in Spain, as the country consolidated its bumpy but successful transition to democracy. Health problems forced James to return to Britain, and from 1983 he lived in Westcliff-on-Sea, Essex, but kept a bag permanently packed for his regular journeys to Spain. Profiled in the Spanish daily, *El País*, Jump's lifestyle and search for new words as he compiled his Penguin dictionary was described as 'the perpetual return'.[78]

By now, James was a true *hispanista*, a proud member of the *tertulia* (discussion group) of poets and artists at the Café Lion in Madrid, taken for a Spaniard whenever in Spain and never more at home than in Spain. But his reports in the weekly *Tribune* newspaper and elsewhere on developments in the country that he loved were sharply critical of the failure to tackle its Francoist legacy of dubious standards in public life and attitudes to women. Typically, one *Tribune* article began: 'Five years ago, when I was living in Spain, I was asked by a London publisher if I could write a school text book with the title *How Spain Is Run*. I replied that I could do it in three words: "Corruptly and inefficiently".' In 1981 his anonymous despatch printed in *Private Eye* delved into the questionable financial affairs of the newly appointed Spanish ambassador in London, Fernando Arias Salgado, while director-general of TVE, Spain's public television broadcaster.[79]

In England, James worked enthusiastically as secretary of the International Brigade Memorial Appeal, which raised the money to erect the magnificent memorial to the International Brigades on London's South Bank. Created by sculptor Ian Walters, it was unveiled by veteran Labour politician Michael Foot in October 1985. James attended the emotionally-charged fiftieth anniversary reunions of International Brigaders from around the world in Madrid in 1986 and then two years later in Barcelona. Around this time he also revised his civil war memoir. A first draft, dated 1966, had been called *Freedom Is Flesh and Blood* (a phrase borrowed from poet Cecil Day Lewis); the second version, which now included several poems, was tagged *Anecdotes from the Spanish Civil War*, with working titles of *The Human Side* or *Oh Yes, We Laughed Sometimes*. Renowned former union leader and fellow International Brigader Jack Jones wrote a foreword for it in 1987 (see page 13). For whatever reason, it remained unpublished.

James R Jump with the maquette for the International Brigade memorial, sculptor Ian Walters (left) and Bill Alexander (right), former British Battalion commander in Spain.

Judged by output, poetry seems to have taken up most of James's creative energies during this final decade of his life. He was the 'house poet' at *Tribune*; three collections of his poems appeared in print and his work featured in anthologies supporting great causes for the left. There was a poem for the miners' strike of 1984/5, *I'm Behind You*, in which he imagines how his friend, Cowdenbeath miner George Jackson, who died in Spain, would have been in the front line of the strike. For an anthology of poems for the Campaign for Nuclear Disarmament, which was undergoing a revival following the government's decision to allow US cruise missiles to be stationed in Britain, Jump contributed *One Woman's Idea of Peace*, in which Prime Minister Margaret Thatcher celebrates a post-nuclear war Britain free of 'CNDers', 'commies' and 'weirdos'.[80]

Some poems he wrote in Spanish only, many in both languages. At the same time as he was re-working his war memoir, James was producing a manuscript of bilingual poems, titled *Poems of War and Peace / Poemas de guerra y de paz*. Leading Spanish playwright Antonio Buero Vallejo wrote an introduction, *El poeta cogió su fusil* (The poet picked up his rifle), in which he said of James and the civil war: 'Only someone who lived through those epic times knows how indelibly they are imprinted on the memory. This is the memory which pulsates through most of the poems in this book.' Years later the collection was published posthumously in Spain.[81]

James R Jump died on 29th November 1990, aged 74. In an obituary in *The Guardian*, Brenda Dean said that Jump's anti-fascism and socialism had been shaped by the political polarisations of the 1930s. 'Injustice and humbug were the enemies,' she wrote and his beliefs had been 'rekindled half a century later by the Thatcher decade'.[82] The print union leader, who had got to know James through her union's support for the International Brigade memorial in central London, noted that he often liked to dwell on the lighter moments of the war in Spain. She went on to repeat one of his favourite stories – which is included in this memoir – about how, on his clandestine journey to Spain, he arrived, as instructed, at the appointed railway station in Paris only to see a hundred other men carrying the identical brown-paper packet of food as his.

'He was never a member of socialism's dour tendency,' Dean added, and pointed to the 'Do Not' plastic card that James had produced in the year before his death. This was to be carried in wallets with an instruction to medical staff not to allow Margaret Thatcher to visit the bearer in the event of being admitted to hospital. 'I do not want anyone to make political capital out of my misfortune,' the card explained. The Thatcher years had seen a spate of tragic transport accidents – the sinking of the ferry *Herald of Free Enterprise* and fire at London's King's Cross station in 1987, a train crash at Clapham Junction in 1988 and the Kegworth air disaster in the following year. The prime minister would invariably be seen on television news visiting survivors in hospital. Sold by Jump via a notice in *Tribune,* which was headed 'Raise two fingers to Maggie!', the card was a runaway success and twice had to be reprinted. Proceeds went to the weekly magazine's fighting fund and to the Labour Party, of which James was now an active member.

My father was many things: journalist, soldier, teacher, writer, linguist, poet, lexicographer, humourist and political activist. The thread that ran through all these manifestations was Spain – the Spaniard he married (Cayetana would survive him for another ten years) and the war that not only determined the course of his life but gave him another 'lifelong love'. Joining the International Brigades was 'something I can feel proud of', he insisted when interviewed a few years before he died, though it had had repercussions on his career. The headmaster at the secondary school where he taught for twelve years had admitted to him that the education authorities in Kent wanted an eye to be kept on his politics. And James pointed out caustically that he had spent thirteen years in higher education – where his college principal referred to him as 'our Red' – and been consistently passed over for promotion.[83]

Sending condolences to the Jump family, Bill Alexander, secretary of the International Brigade Association, wrote: 'With different ideas and philosophy [Jim] could have achieved high status and rewards in the academic or literary fields.' But the course he took in joining the International Brigades 'was the only one at the time for those who cherished humanity and freedom'. The former commander of the British Battalion in Spain concluded: 'Jim's poems and writings will be read and provide inspiration for many years to come.'[84]

Eric Heffer, the redoubtable Labour MP for Liverpool Walton, confessed that he had been moved to tears by reading some of Jump's poems.[85] Quoted in Jump's obituary in *Tribune*, Heffer said: 'Jimmy's experience in Spain greatly influenced the whole of his life, politically and in other ways. It gave him a deep love of Spain and its people and an abiding love of freedom.'[86]

James was buried in the family grave in Wallasey, alongside his twin sister Dorothy, who had died, aged two and a half, in the Spanish flu pandemic of 1919. Draped over his coffin, the red, gold and purple of the Spanish Republic's flag pierced the misty Mersey air, as the plaintive words of *En los pueblos de mi Andalucía*, sung by Anglo-Spanish actor and friend Yolanda Vázquez, rang out across the cemetery.

Thanks

Several people have been of help in editing this memoir, in particular Mike Arnott, Richard Baxell, Ray Hoff, Myra Hunter, Clara Jump, Meirian Jump, the late Sheila Lawler, Carlos Muntión Hernaez, Mark and Mo Newman, Clive Sexton, Marlene Sidaway, Rosita Stefanyszyn and Yolanda Vázquez. Special thanks also go to Simon Deefholts and Kathryn Phillips-Miles at The Clapton Press and to Paul Preston and the late Jack Jones for capturing the essence of my father in their foreword and preface respectively.

Jim Jump is the editor and author of several books on the Spanish Civil War, including *Poems from Spain: British and Irish International Brigaders on the Spanish Civil War* (2006), with Richard Baxell and Angela Jackson: *Antifascistas: British and Irish Volunteers in the Spanish Civil War* (2010) and *Looking Back at the Spanish Civil War* (2010). Since 2002 he has been a trustee of the International Brigade Memorial Trust and is currently its chair.

About the poems

Another Death: First published in *Southend Poetry Broadsheet*, no.3, 1985.

Battle Sounds: First published in *From Britain to Spain and Back: Poems by Jimmy Jump* (London: The John Cornford Poetry Society, 1984).

Before Battle: First published in *From Britain To Spain and Back*, op.cit. The poem was written in Spain in 1938.

British International Brigaders' Reunion: First published in *With Machine Gun and Pen* by James R Jump (Westcliff-on-Sea: Alf Killick Educational Trust, 1990), where it was called 'International Brigaders'. This title is taken from the original manuscript, dated 6th November 1989.

Corpse: First published in *Poems of War and Peace / Poemas de guerra y de paz*, by James R Jump (Logroño: Piedra de Rayo, 2007).

The Deserter: Previously unpublished. The original manuscript is dated 28th August 1987.

Ebro Offensive, 24th July 1938: First published in *Poems from Spain: British and Irish International Brigaders on the Spanish Civil War* edited by Jim Jump (London: Lawrence & Wishart, 2006).

The Fighter Fell in Love: Previously unpublished. The original manuscript is dated 22nd March 1988.

Guard Duty outside Tarazona de la Mancha: Previously unpublished; undated.

If You Had Lived: First published in *Tribune*, 21st October 1983. The poem is one of several that James R Jump wrote about Jackson. *Tribune* published another, *Shared Cigarette,* on 27th October 1989, which it reprinted with Jump's obituary in the magazine on 7th December 1990.

If You Had Seen: Previously unpublished, this poem has been transcribed from the notebook James R Jump kept in Spain.

International Brigaders: First published in *Poems of War and Peace / Poemas de guerra y de paz*, op.cit. Fernando Sanz Compán wrote to James R Jump after reading a letter, published in the *Wallasey and Wirral Chronicle* on 24th September 1938 under the headline 'From a Spanish hospital'.

Lifelong Love: First published in *Poems of War and Peace / Poemas de guerra y de paz*, op.cit.

No-Man's Land: First published in *With Machine Gun and Pen*, op.cit.

Pasionaria: First published in *With Machine Gun and Pen*, op.cit.

The Songs We Sang: First published in *Poems of War and Peace / Poemas de guerra y de paz*, op.cit, the poem was read by James R Jump on the BBC Radio 4 documentary 'Songs of Hope' (produced by Anne Marie Cole and Roy Palmer) about the songs of the British and Irish volunteers in the Spanish Civil War. It was broadcast on 13th July 1986.

Sun over the Front: First published in *With Machine Gun and Pen*, op.cit.

Thoughts on Immortality: First published in *From Britain To Spain and Back*, op.cit.

To a Comrade Sleeping: First published in *With Machine Gun and Pen*, op.cit, the poem was written in 1938 in Spain.

We Cannot Go Back: Previously unpublished, this poem has been transcribed from the notebook James R Jump kept in Spain.

Notes

Glossary of references

ALBA: Abraham Lincoln Brigade Archives database:
https://alba-valb.org/volunteer-database

CCHSCW: Canadian Cultural History about the Spanish Civil
War virtual research environment database:
https://spanishcivilwar.ca/volunteers

IBMT: International Brigade Memorial Trust database:
www.international-brigades.org.uk/the-volunteers

IWM: Imperial War Museum, London

IWMSA: Imperial War Museum Sound Archive, London

JFA: Jump family archive

JRJ: James R Jump

MA: 'Moscow Archive' of digital copies of selected Comintern
records at the Marx Memorial Library (also available online from
RGASPI – see below)

MML: Marx Memorial Library, London

RGASPI: Comintern archives in the Russian State Archive of
Socio-Political History, International Brigade Collection,
Moscow

TNA: The National Archives, Kew

UOB: University of Bristol

[1] IBMT lists Tom Elliott as being killed on the Jarama front, south-east of Madrid, in June 1937. His death was reported in Worthing on 18th September 1937: *Storm Tide: Prelude to War 1933-1939* by Michael Payne (Worthing: Verité CM for Michael Payne, p.127).

[2] Christopher Thornycroft was studying at Brasenose College, Oxford, when he decided to join the International Brigades: *No Other Way: Oxfordshire and the Spanish Civil War* by Chris Farman, Valery Rose and Liz Woolley (Oxford: Oxford International Brigade Memorial Committee, 2015) p.97. Dorothy Thornycroft chaired the Worthing Basque Children's Committee; elder daughter Kate was its secretary and her younger sister Priscilla was active in the Artists International Association in campaigns for the Spanish Republican cause: p.98, ibid.

[3] JRJ twice completed a *Biografía de militantes* in Spain as a member of the Spanish Communist Party. In the first, dated 21st March 1938, he said he had joined the Communist Party in Britain in April 1937, adding that he was a member of its Worthing branch and that he had been expelled from the Labour Party in September 1937 for distributing communist literature; in a second *Biografía*, on 29th November 1938, he said he had joined the party in March 1938. He declared that he was a member of the Communist Party of Great Britain, Labour Party and National Union of Journalists. RGASPI, fond 545, opis 6, delo 156, pp. 23, 24, 27 and 34. JRJ's MI5 file indicates that he was a member of the Communist Party's Wallasey branch (and its press officer) in 1948. The file (TNA, KV 5/125) shows that he was kept under surveillance for many years. His latest accessible record card goes up to 1954, when he was employed by Kent Education Committee.

[4] The interviewer was almost certainly RW 'Robbie' Robson, former London district organiser of the Communist Party, who screened International Brigade volunteers at an office at 1 Litchfield Street in London's Covent Garden: *Unlikely Warriors: The British in the Spanish Civil War and the Struggle Against Fascism* by Richard Baxell (London: Aurum Press, 2012) p.65.

[5] Fernando and Rosa Omegna were the wardens of the homes for Basque refugee children at Beach House, Worthing, and Penstone Park, Lancing; a scrapbook of photos and newspaper cuttings kept by them is held in MML's Spanish Collection (SC/IND/MTG).

6 Now known as the Place du Colonel Fabien, where (at 8 Avenue Mathurin Moreau) a plaque remembering the International Brigades was unveiled in 2011 outside what used to be the central recruiting office: *IBMT Newsletter*, issue 31, New Year 2012.

7 International Exposition of Art and Technology in Modern Life, held in Paris from 25th May to 25th November 1937.

8 Leonard Denny, a blacksmith, was born in 1896. He is listed by IBMT as having deserted or been repatriated from Spain in 1938.

9 The identity of 'Billy' cannot be established from among the 13 other volunteers who arrived in Spain with JRJ on 11th November 1937 and who are described as *inglés* in RGASPI, fond 545, opis 6, delo 35, p.185. None has an obvious Irish connection. There is one 'William': William Henderson, listed as a steel-worker from Calderbank, near Glasgow, who was born in London in 1901; little else is known about him, other than in September 1938 he was a prisoner of Franco: MML MA, disc 2, reel 5, nos.703-704 and IBMT.

10 This was Alexander Calder's installation *Mercury Fountain*, a maquette of which is displayed alongside *Guernica* at the Reina Sofía National Art Museum in Madrid.

11 There were 61 volunteers who, with JRJ, arrived in Spain on 11th November 1937, having crossed the Pyrenees by foot via Massanet de Cabrenys; they included men of 11 different nationalities: RGASPI, fond 545, opis 6, delo 35, p.185, including six Americans. Who was 'Larry'? ALBA lists one of the six as being from Milwaukee, 21-year-old Mike Bubich, who had sailed on the *President Roosevelt*. Lawrence Wendorf, aged 23, of Milwaukee, who, according to ALBA, sailed on the *Britannic*, later appears to have been a colleague or associate of the Tarazona training camp HQ staff in January 1938. Along with JRJ and others pictured on page 64, 'Larry Wendorf' signed a souvenir address book kept by Cyril Sexton (in the Sexton family archives) with the message: 'Looking forward to a swell time together in London'. In JRJ's recollections, could 'Larry' be a composite character of more than one of the Americans he came across?

12 Non-intervention in the Spanish Civil War was the collective policy promoted by Britain and France from August 1936 and supported by all

European governments under the Non-Intervention Agreement. 'By applying an arms embargo on both sides in the war, it discriminated against the Spanish Republic and in favour of the military rebels, who continued to receive support from Germany and Italy.': Enrique Moradiellos in 'Albion's Perfidy: The British Government and the Spanish Civil War' in *Looking Back at the Spanish Civil War* edited by Jim Jump (London: Lawrence & Wishart, 2010) p.95.

[13] Harry Pollitt (1890-1960) was the general secretary of the Communist Party of Great Britain. Lady (Nancy) Astor (1879-1964) was a Conservative MP and leading member of the 'Cliveden Set', a group of politically influential people who in the 1930s favoured friendly relations with Nazi Germany.

[14] Alex McDade's last line of this verse was: 'And most of our old age as well'. For his original version see *British Volunteers for Liberty: Spain 1936-39* by Bill Alexander (London: Lawrence & Wishart, 1982) pp.106-7.

[15] *La Pasionaria* (passion flower) was Dolores Ibárruri (1895-1989), a leading wartime cabinet minister, communist deputy in the Spanish parliament (Cortes) and fiery orator.

[16] The 'artificial exchange rate' at the time, JRJ recalled 40 years later in *The Distant Drum: Reflections on the Spanish Civil War* edited by Philip Toynbee (London: Sidgwick and Jackson, 1976) p.116, was 40 pesetas to the pound.

[17] Herman Engert, according to ALBA, was a German American from New York.

[18] Sung to the tune of the Russian military song *White Army, Black Baron*: p.320 in *Merriman's Diaries: Exegesis* edited by Raymond M Hoff (digitally hosted by the Tamiment Library, New York University, 2018).

[19] JRJ later recalled that it was Alvah Bessie, from the Cultural Commission, who suggested that he should contribute towards the wall newspaper and become a clerk-interpreter at camp headquarters in Tarazona. Bessie was 'very enthusiastic about everything – a light seemed to shine in his eyes': interviewed in 1986, IWMSA 9524/6, reel 2. ALBA's biography of Bessie describes how he was later sacked as a

Hollywood screen writer for his communist sympathies and became one of the Hollywood Ten, refusing to answer questions about his or other people's political affiliations; in 1951 he was gaoled for 11 months.

20 Cipriano Escudero Salido was the senior Spanish commander in the British Battalion (November 1937 list of officers: RGASPI, fond 545, opus 2, delo 109, p.131), who, in October 1938, as Captain Cipriano, assumed overall command following the withdrawal of the British and other foreign volunteers; p.273 and p.346 in Baxell, *Unlikely Warriors*, op.cit.

21 Frank Deegan, from Bootle, was a Liverpool docker who, according to IBMT, arrived in Spain in June 1937 and returned home with the British Battalion in December 1938.

22 The base clerk at Tarazona at the time was Al Handler, also known as Al Stanley, who is listed as being an oil worker with an address in Philadelphia: RGASPI, fond 545, opis 2, del, 260, p.51 and ALBA.

23 William Durston, a diecaster originally from Aberaman, near Aberdare, but living in Wembley before going to Spain, was killed in September 1938 in the Sierra de Caballs during the Battle of the Ebro: IBMT and *David HJ Newman in Spain 1937-38: David Henry James Newman's experience in the Spanish Civil War* edited by Mark and Mo Newman (Blurb UK: 2012) p.103.

24 George Edgar's real name was Edgar Lemkc, aged 54. According to CCHSCW, Lemke was reported to be the oldest serving Canadian volunteer and spoke English, Russian, German, Spanish, French and Norwegian.

25 CCHSCW; JRJ gives Ouellette's name as Jean-François in his manuscripts.

26 This could be William 'Bill' Beeching, who, according to CCHSCW, was an accountant from Regina, Saskatchewan, or Hendrick 'Henry' Oraschuk, from Edmonton, Alberta, who also signed Cyril Sexton's address book (see note 11).

27 The *Ciudad de Barcelona* was torpedoed by an Italian submarine off the Spanish coast after setting sail from Marseilles on 30th May 1937. Some 50 of the more than 250 International Brigade volunteers on

board lost their lives: *Odyssey of the Lincoln Brigade: Americans in the Spanish Civil War* by Peter N Carroll (Stanford: Stanford University Press, 1994) p.125. In *David HJ Newman in Spain 1937-38*, op.cit, p.26, Dave Newman was taken ashore with other survivors to the nearby coastal town of Malgrat de Mar, where the barracks were converted into a makeshift hospital.

28 Allan Johnson was the *nom de guerre* of Allan McNeil, Glasgow-born former US Army officer. His home town was Boston, according to ALBA, though JRJ's notebook in Spain has an address for him in New York's East 13th Street. As a communist, McNeil faced deportation hearings during the McCarthy witch-hunts, which lasted 13 years until McNeil's death in 1966. He complained: 'The attempt of our government to go to bed with butcher Franco . . . requires that they silence all opposition to their pro-fascist drive.': p.296 in Carroll, *The Odyssey of the Abraham Lincoln Brigade*, op.cit. JRJ later recalled that Johnson was 'a bit of a disciplinarian' and wouldn't stand slackness, whether lateness for training, carelessness in handling weapons or slowness to dig-in when on manoeuvres: interviewed in 1986, IWMSA, 9524/6, reel 2.

29 Probably battalion postman Rowland Williams, a miner from Trelewis in the Rhondda, who was wounded in the hip during the Battle of Brunete in July 1937: MML MA, disc 5, reel 10, nos. 753-754.

30 Listed by ALBA as Marshall García Menéndez.

31 The Assault Guard was an urban police force created by the Spanish Republic in 1931 and disbanded by Franco in 1939.

32 Charlotte Haldane chaired the International Brigades' Dependants and Wounded Aid Committee, which was created in June 1937 to raise funds for the welfare of widows and bereaved families of International Brigade volunteers: *Britain and the Spanish Civil War* by Tom Buchanan (Cambridge: Cambridge University Press, 1997) p.142.

33 Bill Harrington saw action at the Battle of the Ebro in the summer of 1938 as a sergeant of no.2 company of the British Battalion; at Hill 481 on 30th July, after company commander John Angus and his second-in-command were injured, Harrington took over the command, only to be wounded himself: p.207 in Alexander, *British Volunteers for Liberty*, op.cit.

34 Literally a 'plugged-in' person.

35 According to Alexander, pp.81-82 in *British Volunteers for Liberty*, op.cit, 298 of the volunteers made their way back to Britain. Some justified their action with 'horror stories', while others were 'emotionally and physically exhausted, or mentally unsuitable for modern warfare'. A few men returned to Spain: *British Volunteers in the Spanish Civil War: The British Battalion in the International Brigades, 1936-1939* by Richard Baxell (London: Routledge, 2004) p.140.

36 This could be YCL member George Robertson from Carrick Knowe Road, Edinburgh, who arrived in Spain on 22nd November 1937 and returned home on 25th October 1938. Was he the son of Rev Andrew Robertson, minister for Prestonfield in Edinburgh from 1926-1937? MML docs.6534, box no.79/4/1 and *Fasti Ecclesiae Scoticanae: The Succession Of Ministers In The Church Of Scotland From The Reformation*, vol.8, p.14.

37 Joe Sloane, a chauffeur, arrived in Spain in December 1936, took part in the Battle of Jarama two months later and was afterwards based in Tarazona as a driver; at his request he returned home from Vilaseca in May 1938: MML MA, disc 3, reel 9, nos.661-664.

38 Franco's forces had arrived in Vinaroz on 15th April 1938, thereby cutting Republican territory in two.

39 The Servicio de Investigación Militar (SIM) was the secret police of the Spanish Republic's armed forces, created in August 1937 under the guidance of the Soviet NKVD: *Novedad en el frente: las Brigadas Internacionales en la guerra civil* by Rémi Skoutelsky (Madrid: Temas de Hoy, 2006) pp.345-346.

40 Rémi Skoutelsky, p.355, ibid, goes along with J Delperrié de Bayac's estimate in *Les Brigades Internationales* (Paris: Marabout, 1985) that throughout the war about 50 International Brigaders of all nationalities were executed for various reasons. More recent studies give a higher, three-figure estimate, especially when battlefield executions for desertion are factored in: see *Fighting for Spain: The International Brigades in the Civil War, 1936-1949* by Alexander Clifford (Barnsley: Pen & Sword Military, 2020) p.46.

41 Jack Nalty, according to IBMT, fought in the no.1 company, 14th

Brigade, at Córdoba in December 1936, was sent back to Ireland in the summer of 1937 and returned to Spain in April 1938.

[42] Tom (Thomas) Murray was a farmworker from Edinburgh, whose brother George was serving in the 15th Brigade's Anti-Tank Battery and sister Anne was a nurse in Spain: p.45 in Baxell, *British Volunteers in the Spanish Civil War*, op.cit. Murray was a Labour councillor in the city, while at the same time a secret member of the Communist Party: *Into the Heart of the Fire: The British in the Spanish Civil War* by James K Hopkins (Stanford: Stanford University Press, 1998) p.251.

[43] The French authorities interned half a million Spaniards escaping Franco's forces in a network of concentration camps in and around Saint-Cyprien and in other sites close to the Spanish border. The refugees were kept in inhumane conditions, mostly on sand dunes, enclosed by barbed wire, without shelter and with little food and drinking water: *The Spanish Civil War*, third edition, by Hugh Thomas (Harmondsworth: Penguin Books, 1977) p.878.

[44] Others have been given credit for this display of machine gun prowess, including Paddy O'Sullivan and Maurice Ryan: *At the Margins of Mayhem: Prologue and Epilogue to the Last Great Battle of the Spanish Civil War* by Angela Jackson (Pontypool: Warren & Pell, 2008) p.90.

[45] The incident is described in more detail in *Brigadista: An Irishman's Fight against Fascism* by Bob Doyle (Dublin: Curragh Press, 2006) pp.83-4. Doyle recounts that the prisoners, in the first week of September 1938, were issued with a khaki shirt, a pair of breeches and canvas shoes especially for Lady (Ivy Muriel) Chamberlain's visit.

[46] The photo was published in the *Liverpool Echo* on 21st July 1938, with a report of the visit to the British Battalion by George Bean, president of the Liverpool Guild of Students and vice-president of the National Union of Students. The photo's caption contained several errors, highlighted in 'Who's pictured here before the Battle of the Ebro?', *IBMT Newsletter*, issue 36, 1-2014.

[47] Gordon Bennett, a tyre moulder, was killed on 26th July 1938. His brother David, listed as a furnace-man, returned home on 1st September 1938: IBMT.

48 General Eoin O'Duffy, leader of Ireland's fascist Blueshirts, recruited 700 Irishmen for the XV Bandera of the Spanish Foreign Legion: *Franco's International Brigades: Foreign Volunteers and Fascist Dictators in the Spanish Civil War* by Christopher Othen (London: Reportage Press, 2008) p.115.

49 Maurice Ryan was executed on 5th August 1938 by British Battalion commander Sam Wild and his adjutant, George Fletcher, not for 'Trotskyism' but after being found guilty of turning his machine gun on his own comrades in the Sierra de Caballs during the Battle of the Ebro: pp.258-260, Baxell in *Unlikely Warriors*, op.cit. Hopkins, in *Into the Heart of the Fire*, pp.266-67, op.cit, quotes Tom Murray, who said Ryan showed disobedience on the battlefield by refusing to relocate his gun and threatening Murray with a grenade, for which he was immediately demoted. He was subsequently discovered to have a brother serving with the enemy and to be from an anti-Soviet and anti-socialist background. Many years later JRJ wrote a poem, *M... R..., Fifty Years On*, published in *With Machine Gun and Pen*, by James R Jump (Westcliff-on-Sea: Alf Killick Educational Trust, 1990) p.30, recalling their friendship: *You died ignominiously – / a hastily convened court-martial / and a ragged volley / fired by your former comrades. / Your corpse was unceremoniously / dumped in an unmarked grave / but you are no worse off than the brave / who died heroically. / Their bones, / once marked by standing stones, / were dug up and scattered / when Franco won the war. / Though I do not condone / what you did, Paddy, / I cannot forget our friendship. / There were times when your sense of fun / did more to keep up our morale / than all the slogans and sermonising / of our political commissars. / What is more, you were a fine machine gunner / when you were not / sleeping off the effects of drunkenness.*

50 Rumoured to be a descendent of Clive of India, Lewis Clive was educated at Eton and Christ Church, Oxford, and had been a member of the British gold-medal team at the Los Angeles Olympics in 1932: Farman, Rose and Woolley in *No Other Way* p.63, op.cit. Baxell in *British Volunteers in the Spanish Civil War*, p.15, op.cit, says Clive was also a member of the Communist Party at the same time as being a Labour councillor. He died on 1st August 1938: IBMT.

51 IBMT records show that David Guest, killed on 26th July 1938, had only enlisted in the International Brigades in May of that year, following

his sister Angela, who had arrived two months earlier. JRJ said of Guest in 1986, IWMSA 9524/6, reel 2: 'I got on well with him, perhaps he was my type – didn't go drinking and would prefer to sit around and talk about politics or literature.'

52 John Smith was, according to IBMT, a miner and already a Communist Party member, suggesting that the 'drink, women and loot' boast may have been a piece of bravado on the part of a young man. An assessment by Lieutenant Arthur Olorenshaw in Smith's personal files describes him as an 'Excellent soldier... Good militant type, inclined to drink but has... retained good record in the Line'. He was killed on 8th September 1938 in the Sierra de Caballs and had been injured a few weeks earlier in fighting in the Sierra de Pandols on 17th August: MML MA, disc 4, reel 9, nos.779-781.

53 Jansen Van Orren is listed in 1938 as a 30-year-old Londoner: MML MA, disc 5, reel 10, no.296. On p.113 of Toynbee, *A Distant Drum*, op.cit, JRJ suggests that Van Orren was a deserter from the Household Cavalry and had 'no very strong political views' when he left Britain.

54 JRJ in 1986 recalled, IWMSA 9524/6, reel 5, how George Jackson, despite their different backgrounds and ages, seemed to 'take me under his wing and we used to talk for hours. He would be talking about his life in the pit and he'd be asking me questions about my life as a newspaper reporter.' IBMT reports that Jackson was killed on 19th August 1938.

55 According to CCHSCW, Florence Pike was one of only two Canadian women enrolled in the International Brigades.

56 Dubliner William McGregor and Jack Nalty, from Galway, were, according to IBMT, killed on the British Battalion's last day of action, 23rd September 1938, and received posthumous citations for bravery.

57 '57th (British) Battalion', *Daily Worker*, 31st August 1938.

58 Dave Newman expressed this sense of incredulity in a letter to his mother and father on 23rd September 1938: 'It was rather a surprise and you can guess how anxious we were to read the news ourselves... [Dr Negrín's] speech is, as you can imagine, the main topic of conversation. Things like bacon and egg for breakfast seem like dreams now. But there was one thing which no one can quite understand – the reason for such action by the Govt. They weren't compelled to do so and

there doesn't seem to be a sufficiently large reason for it.': *David HJ Newman in Spain: 1937-38*, op.cit, p.85.

[59] Another of the casualties was Lieutenant Alec Cummings, a lecturer from Cardiff, under whom JRJ had worked in Albacete. His precise fate remains uncertain. He was reported to have been killed in action but there remains speculation that he was executed for desertion: *Wales and the Spanish Civil War: The Dragon's Dearest Cause?* by Robert Stradling (Cardiff: University of Wales Press, 2004) pp.147-50.

[60] A total of 305 members of the British Battalion left Spain on 6th December 1938: p.140 in Buchanan, *Britain and the Spanish Civil War* op.cit. However, 75 British and Irish prisoners remained in the San Pedro de Cardeña prison camp, with the last Briton repatriated in March 1940: pp.128-29, Baxell in *British Volunteers in the Spanish Civil War*, op.cit.

[61] JRJ interviewed in 1986, IWMSA, 9524/6, reel 1.

[62] Letter from Geoffrey Fisher, Bishop of Chester, to the Rev KV Evelyn-White, 15th February 1936, JFA; and 'Hail, Caesar: Journalist's Passion Play', *Wallasey and Wirral Chronicle*, 18th April 1936.

[63] JRJ interviewed in 1986, IWMSA, 9524/6, reel 1. John 'Jack' Davies Jump (1914-1976) completed postgraduate studies at Liverpool University in 1936 and in the following year was appointed assistant lecturer at Manchester University, eventually becoming Professor of English Literature in 1965: obituary in *The Times,* 1st July 1976: 'Professor JD Jump: Scholar and editor'.

[64] JRJ wrote the front-page report in the *Worthing Herald* of 18th July 1936 headlined: 'In the End Justice Will Conquer: Emperor's Conviction: Statement to Herald', based on an interview that he conducted with Haile Selassie's press attaché; this was also the day that the attempted coup d'état was launched on the Spanish mainland, thereby triggering the civil war.

[65] JRJ interviewed in 1986, IWMSA, 9524/6, reel 1. Up to 1,800 Republican prisoners were executed after General Yagüe's rebel forces occupied Badajoz on 14th August 1936: p.371 in Thomas, *The Spanish Civil War*, op.cit.

[66] Cayetana wrote about her first return trip to Spain in 'Living in Spain Today', *Daily Worker*, 25th October 1946.

[67] Letters from Cayetana Jump, 'Forgotten men', *Sunday Post*, 16th September 1945 and 'Spanish Prisoners', *Lancashire Evening Post*, 30th October 1945.

[68] Payne, p.216, in *Storm Tide*, op.cit, and in 'Behind the Counter at Spain Shop', *Worthing Herald*, 10th March 1939, and 'Help for Spain', *Worthing Gazette*, 29th March 1939.

[69] 'The Struggle in Spain', p.239, *The Wallaseyan*, April 1939.

[70] A draft of the memoir dated 1966 is in the IWM: Interwar Private Papers, JR Jump, Documents. 11089. The University of Bristol Information Office's *Newsletter* of 30th May 1974, vol.4 no.17, p.3, 'Gift to library', reports that John (sic) R Jump 'has now written up his diary of his experiences [in Spain] and presented to the Library the manuscript and a collection of books, pamphlets and other material from that period. In the collection are popular ballads, reminiscences of the poet, Antonio Machado, and propaganda material of great interest... A small poster commemorating "One Year of Battle" of the XV Brigade bears the signature of Paul Robeson.' Sadly, the manuscript, books, pamphlets and signed poster cannot be found by the library, though its Special Collections still holds some postcards and ephemera, including a red cap badge: UOB, DM1501.

[71] *La ofensiva del Ebro* by James R Jump (London: Harrap, 1975).

[72] Letter from Philip Toynbee to JRJ, 2nd April 1975, JFA.

[73] 'Our Hearts Were Young and Gay', p.114, *New Statesman*, 23rd July 1976.

[74] *The Spaniard and his Language* by James R Jump (London: Harrap, 1951).

[75] *The Penguin Spanish Dictionary* compiled by James R Jump (London: Penguin Books, 1990).

[76] 'International Exhibition of Children's Art', p.7, *The Templar*, 1955.

77 'Spanish Rugby Football Terminology', *Vida Hispánica*, Winter 1974; 'Modern Spanish nursery rhymes', *Modern Languages*, October 1954; 'Two hundred years of Spanish grammars', *Modern Languages*, March 1961; 'Spain's Changing Imperative?', *Linguists' Review*, June 1959; 'The rehabilitation of Vicente Blasco Ibáñez', *Modern Languages*, September 1967; 'Pilgrimage to Fuentevaqueros', *Modern Languages*, March 1963; 'La Cordoniz: Speaking out in a totalitarian society', *Modern Languages*, September 1975.

78 'Jimmy Jump: El perpetuo regreso a España en busca de palabras', *El País*, 19th November 1988.

79 'Jobs for the boys – but only one each', *Tribune*, 29th June 1984; 'Letter from Madrid', *Private Eye*, 24th April, 1981.

80 *Against All the Odds* edited by Maurice Jones (Barnsley: National Union of Mineworkers, 1984) p.4; *Poems for Peace* edited by Linda Hoy (London: Pluto Press, 1986) p.32.

81 *Poems of War and Peace / Poemas de guerra y de paz* by James R Jump (Logroño: Piedra de Rayo, 2007); Buero Vallejo quotation on p.10.

82 'James Jump: for Spanish and the Republic', *The Guardian*, 7th December 1990.

83 JRJ interviewed in 1986, IWMSA, 9524/6, reel 6.

84 Letter from Bill Alexander to Jim Jump on 2nd December 1990, JFA.

85 Introduction to *With Machine Gun and Pen*, op.cit., by James R Jump, (Westcliff-on-Sea: Alf Killick Educational Trust, 1990).

86 'Jimmy Jump: 1916-1990', *Tribune*, 7th December 1990.

Index

British Battalion (see International Brigades)
Browder, Earl 38, 116
Brunete 25, 45, 194
Bubich, Mike 191

Calder, Alexander 191
Calderbank 191
Canadian Mounted Police (Royal) 64
Cardiff 199
Catalonia, flag 123-126
Catholic Church 106
Cayetana (see Lozano Díaz)
Cervera 105
Chamberlain, Lady (Ivy Muriel) 117, 196
Chamberlain, Neville 30, 38
Christ Church College, Oxford 197
Church of Scotland 84
Cipriano, Lieutenant 61, 193
Ciudad de Barcelona 65, 193-194
Clive, Lewis 135, 197
Cliveden Set 192
Coimbra University 84
Committee for Spanish Relief 87
Communist Party
– of Great Britain 22, 109, 134, 190, 192
– French: Parti Communiste 172
– Spanish 59, 70, 117, 190, 192
– US 38, 116
– Young Communist League (YCL) 134, 195
Cooney, Bob 107-108, 140, 168
Corbera 125-127, 131, 136
Córdoba 196
Cowdenbeath 143
Cummings, Alec 80, 82, 85, 86, 87, 98, 199

Daily Worker 150, 198
De Valera Éamon 134
Deegan, Frank 61, 193
Denny, Leonard 25, 30, 36, 191
Dioppe 172
Don Quijote 82, 161
Doyle, Bob 117, 196

Murray, Tom 108-109, 113-114, 121-125, 131, 132, 139, 143, 147, 151, 168, 196, 197

Nalty, Jack 108, 113-114, 122, 124-126, 128, 131, 132, 150-151, 158, 195, 198
National Union of Journalists 190
National Union of Students 117, 196
Negrín, Juan 86, 153, 198
Nehru, Jawaharlal Pandit 116-117
New Statesman 134
New York 38, 63, 157, 192, 194
Newhaven 172
Newman, Dave 64-65, 149-150, 157-158, 160, 161, 162, 167-168, 170, 194, 198-199
News Chronicle 82, 138
NKVD (Soviet secret police) 195
Non-Intervention Committee 39, 78, 158, 172, 191-192

O'Duffy, Eoin 134, 197
Olorenshaw, Arthur 198
Omegna, Fernando and Rosa 23, 190
Ontañón, Eduardo de 116
Oraschuk, Henry 193
Orihuela 116
O'Sullivan, Paddy 63, 98, 103, 133, 135, 196
Ouellette, Germain 64, 193

Paris
– Gare de Lyon 32-33
– Gare du Nord 28, 30
– International Brigade recruitment centre 28-30, 32, 191
– International Exhibition 25, 26, 30-32
Paris (Ontario) 149
Pasionaria, La (see Ibárruri)
Philadelphia 193
Picasso, Pablo 31
Pike, Florence 149, 198
Pimple, the (see Hill 481)
Planas, Las 166-168
Pollitt, Harry 45, 67, 109, 192
Ponce, Juan 65, 66, 73
POUM, Partido Obrero de Unificación Marxista 47

Poveda, Jesús 115-116
Power, Johnny 168-169, 171, 173
President Roosevelt 191
Puigcerdá 168, 172
Pyrenees
– Crossing by foot 38-41, 191
– Mountains 23, 36, 169

Queen Mary 32, 37

RAF (Royal Air Force) 78
Ramón, Captain 66
Regina (Saskatchewan) 193
Reus 100, 101
Rhondda 170, 194
Ripoll 168-172
Robertson, Andrew 195
Robertson, George 195
Robeson, Paul 60
Robson, RW 'Robbie' 190
Roda, La 54
Roosevelt, Franklin 38
Royal Navy 159
Ruiz Vilaplana, Antonio 32
Ryan, Maurice 'Paddy' 134-135, 196,197

Saint-Cyprien 116, 196
Salvation Army 172
San Pedro de Cardeña 117, 199
Sancho Panza 161
Santa Coloma de Farnés (see Hospitals: Farnés de la Selva)
Sanz Compán, Fernando 161
Schultz, Elias 157
Second World War 74, 116, 134, 170
Seeger, Pete 138
Servicio de Investigación Militar (SIM) 102, 195
Sexton, Cyril 64, 191, 193
Sierra de Caballs 131, 139, 193, 197, 198
Sierra de Pandols 140, 198
Sinclair, Upton 38
Sloane, Joe 97, 100, 195
Smith, John 114, 136, 150-151, 198

Also available from The Clapton Press:

NEVER MORE ALIVE:
INSIDE THE SPANISH REPUBLIC
by Kate Mangan with a preface by Paul Preston

When her lover, the German refugee Jan Kurzke, made his way to Spain to join the International Brigade in October 1936, Kate Mangan went after him. She ended up working with Constancia de la Mora in the Republic's Press Office, where she met a host of characters including WH Auden, Stephen Spender, Ernest Hemingway, Robert Capa, Gerda Taro and many more. When Jan was seriously injured she visited him in hospital, helped him across the border to France and left him with friends in Paris so she could return to her job in Valencia.

This first edition includes a Preface by Paul Preston, an Afterword by Kate's daughter, Charlotte Kurzke, and a note on certain key Comintern agents in Spain by Dr Boris Volodarsky.

theclaptonpress.com

Also available from The Clapton Press:

FIRING A SHOT FOR FREEDOM: THE MEMOIRS OF FRIDA STEWART with a Foreword and Afterword by Angela Jackson
Frida Stewart drove an ambulance to Murcia to help the Spanish Republic and visited the front in Madrid. During the Second World War she was arrested by the Gestapo in Paris and escaped from her internment camp with help from the French Resistance, returning to London where she worked with General de Gaulle. This is her previously unpublished memoir.

BRITISH WOMEN AND THE SPANISH CIVIL WAR by Angela Jackson – 2020 Edition
Angela Jackson's classic examination of the interaction between British women and the war in Spain, through their own oral and written narratives. Revised and updated for this new edition.

BOADILLA by Esmond Romilly
The nephew that Winston Churchill disowned describes his experiences fighting with the International Brigade to defend the Spanish Republic. Written on his honeymoon in France after he eloped with Jessica Mitford.

MY HOUSE IN MALAGA by Sir Peter Chalmers Mitchell
While most ex-pats fled to Gibraltar in 1936, Sir Peter stayed on to protect his house and servants from the rebels. He ended up in prison for sheltering Arthur Koestler from Franco's rabid head of propaganda, who had threatened to 'shoot him like a dog'.

SPANISH PORTRAIT by Elizabeth Lake
A brutally honest, semi-autobiographical novel set in San Sebastián and Madrid between 1934 and 1936, portraying a frantic love affair against a background of confusion and apprehension as Spain drifted inexorably towards civil war.

SOME STILL LIVE by F.G. Tinker Jr.
Frank Tinker was a US pilot who signed up with the Republican forces because he didn't like Mussolini. He was also attracted by the prospect of adventure and a generous pay cheque. This is an account of his experiences in Spain.

theclaptonpress.com

Lightning Source UK Ltd.
Milton Keynes UK
UKHW020632130421
381918UK00013B/886